Action Research
in the Classroom

Action Research in the Classroom

Helping Teachers Assess and Improve their Work

Sr. Mary Ann Jacobs
and Bruce S. Cooper

ROWMAN & LITTLEFIELD
Lanham • Boulder • New York • London

Published by Rowman & Littlefield
A wholly owned subsidiary of The Rowman & Littlefield Publishing Group, Inc.
4501 Forbes Boulevard, Suite 200, Lanham, Maryland 20706
www.rowman.com

Unit A, Whitacre Mews, 26-34 Stannary Street, London SE11 4AB

British Library Cataloguing in Publication Information Available

Library of Congress Cataloging-in-Publication Data

Names: Jacobs, Mary Ann, Sister, author. | Cooper, Bruce S., author.
Title: Action research in the classroom : helping teachers assess and improve their work / Sister Mary Ann Jacobs and Bruce S. Cooper.
Description: Lanham : Rowman & Littlefield, [2016]
Identifiers: LCCN 2015050854 (print) | LCCN 2016007248 (ebook) | ISBN 9781475820935 (cloth : alk. paper) | ISBN 9781475820942 (pbk. : alk. paper) | ISBN 9781475820959 (Electronic)
Subjects: LCSH: Action research in education. | Teachers—In-service training.
Classification: LCC LB1028.24 .J33 2016 (print) | LCC LB1028.24 (ebook) | DDC 370.72—dc23
LC record available at http://lccn.loc.gov/2015050854

∞™ The paper used in this publication meets the minimum requirements of American National Standard for Information Sciences—Permanence of Paper for Printed Library Materials, ANSI/NISO Z39.48-1992.

Printed in the United States of America

Contents

Preface   vii

Part I. Understanding the Process   1

1   Improving Teacher Preparation and Practices   3

2   Understanding Teachers and Improving Life in the Classroom   17

3   Principals' Role in Supporting Research and Improving
Practices for New Teachers   31

Part II. Six Steps in the Process of *L.E.A.D.E.R.*   47

4   Building a Program for Teachers and Students: Six Steps
to Becoming a Classroom *L.E.A.D.E.R.*   49

5   Looking at the Problem   61

6   Examining What's Known   73

7   Acquiring New Knowledge through Action Research   85

8   Devising Plans for School Improvement: Action Research
in Action   95

9   Executing and Evaluating the Plan: How to Start and Make
It Work   111

10   Repeating the Steps as Needed: Helping Teachers Implement
Change and Share Findings   123

Part III. Practical Applications of Action Research   139

11 Samples and Examples of Action Research   141

12 Research on the Research: What Works in Action Research
and What Pitfalls to Avoid   157

Index   171

About the Authors   181

Preface

Teaching has been in my blood since I was six years old. I was one of those children who played school with my dolls, and on occasion with my brothers, when I could coax them into sitting in my basement classroom, listening to my directives, and filling out worksheets I made. I loved it, and the love only grew when I had my first class of first-graders and then just about every level thereafter up to the present day, preparing teacher candidates for the most wonderful vocation and profession—yes, profession—one can enter. The years of teaching have been my instructors. My only regret is that the many lessons learned are stored in memory—which is wonderful for me but of little benefit to other teachers.

I did not know I was an action researcher with that specified designation. I was, after all, just a teacher who never tired of finding new ways to provide more learning for more students in more ways more of the time.

I first met Bruce when he was writing his fortieth or forty-first book, *Mentoring for Meaning*. He invited me to write a chapter for the book on mentoring in Catholic schools. That chapter led to the invitation to write our own book—my choice. I was honored and humbled to work with a prolific teacher and writer—one who regarded his retirement as another teaching opportunity to help me write the book I wanted.

As a teacher, I have always been the practitioner. I had to have a reason for learning, for writing, for experimenting and inquiring. I was the logical sequential representing about 20 percent of the population—the percent that make up about 80 percent of teachers. The logical sequential is best situated for teaching teachers—those who often learn as logical sequentials. These sequentials do not necessarily make the best teachers, as we tend to teach as we learn. But we do make great writers.

Thus the idea was born for this book. Centuries have passed with incredible teachers ingeniously touching minds and hearts. No scientist, doctor, lawyer, or other regarded professional practices today without the influence of a teacher. Rarely do these certified professionals recount the academic journey that brought them to where they are today.

Teachers have been perfecting a craft for centuries and continue to do so. Teachers are researchers in action. Their professional craft continuously evolves as they daily meet and respond to the challenges of making learning happen for young people. The time has come for teacher researchers to capture their craft in writing and share that craft with their professional colleagues.

Our goal in writing this book is to help new and nearly new teachers and seasoned teachers new to action research to recognize themselves as action researchers and to share their findings with the teaching community. New teachers (those just entering the field) and nearly new (those who are close to becoming teachers and those who have been teaching for a few years) as well as those veteran teachers new to action research are the intended audience for this book. Additionally, those who work with these new and nearly new teachers—mentors, principals, assistant principals, department chairs, professors preparing teachers, colleagues in the field—are beneficiaries of this book on using action research to improve teaching and learning.

This book is meant to be a reference guide for new and nearly new teachers, veteran teachers, and those who work with them to easily assist them in developing, following, and sharing their learning in classrooms across the world. The six-step *L.E.A.D.E.R.* model, designed by teachers for teachers, will help teachers look at problems they face in their classrooms, examine what they know about those problems, acquire new knowledge to help them solve those problems, devise and execute a research plan to solve the problem, and repeat the steps in the problem where necessary to lead learning.

Before reading this book, teachers and those who work with them will think that action research is another form of research conducted by those who have time to read and write about the research of others. After reading this book, teachers and those who work with them will see that action research is the work of teachers in classrooms who daily seek and find ways to provide more learning for more students in more ways more of the time, and who take responsibility to share those findings with other professionals in the field.

For apart from inquiry, apart from the praxis, individuals cannot be truly human. Knowledge emerges only through invention and re-invention, through the restless, impatient, continuing, hopeful inquiry human beings pursue in the world, with the world, and with each other.

—*Paulo Freire, Pedagogy of the Oppressed* (1970)

Teachers in action make this happen.

I

UNDERSTANDING THE PROCESS

Teachers can become more professional and effective by working together in a supportive environment. Somehow they need to break out of the classroom, communicate with each other (electronically and in person), share their problems and their best lessons and experiences, and promote their favorite and best classes.

This first section addresses how teachers can improve their teaching and their lives beginning with their training as a first-year teacher, based on "action research." Teachers view teaching as a profession even though they may not yet work together as a professional team. Key to the process is mutual leadership among the teachers as well as hierarchical leadership within the school and school district. Everyone should work together for the common good. Steps are necessary to build and support a program for school administrators, teachers, and even students, to work together to lead learning with high standards and collegiality using action research.

1

Improving Teacher Preparation and Practices

Celebrating the successful completion of a teacher education degree at graduation is truly wonderful. Yet many new teachers, sadly, reach the classroom without adequate training, experience, or know-how on how to test, analyze, and improve their own practices. As Eileen Ferrance (2000) in her book, *Themes in Education: Action Research*, explains:

> Typically, action research is undertaken in a school setting. It is a reflective process that allows for inquiry and discussion as components of the "research." Often, action research is a collaborative activity among colleagues searching for solutions to everyday, real problems experienced in schools, or looking for ways to improve instruction and increase student achievement. Rather than dealing with the theoretical, action research allows practitioners to address those concerns that are closest to them, ones over which they can exhibit some influence and make change. (introduction)

Teachers need ways to analyze student learning, explore options for increasing student growth, and ultimately improve their practices.

DANICA'S STORY

Danica was completing field hours for her final education course with twelfth-grade students in English class with the same group with whom she had completed her student teaching experience the previous semester. Part of her assignment was to work with those high school students in need of reading or writing assistance. These students were reading *The Kite Runner*.

While student teaching, Danica noticed students' low performance on quizzes, papers, discussions, and homework assignments. Initially she believed that these students either did not care to study as much as needed, or they did not understand what was being asked of them. When she visited them again in their final semester of high school, she observed that although some students took notes, they didn't know how to take them effectively. Other students took enough notes only to satisfy the teacher. Through conversations with students, she discovered the root of the problem was no one had ever taught these students how to take notes.

After observing students and consulting with their teacher, Danica set a plan in motion to help these soon-to-be college students learn note taking. The first day was dedicated to describing the process and sharing experiences students had with note taking. Students were asked to list any note-taking strategies that they used. Generic answers were given, such as highlighting, circling words and/or phrases, annotating, and abbreviating.

The students were then asked if they constantly used those strategies and if they believed the strategies were helpful. Collectively, students agreed that they in fact did not implement those strategies regularly, and they were not convinced the strategies were helpful. Danica shared facts and data on how successful note taking could improve students' overall learning experience.

Danica collected note-taking samples from the students to evaluate how they took notes and how well developed the notes were. She found many samples were incomplete and unfocused. Main ideas were missing, and there was no structure in the notes. Based on this information, she chose two structured note-taking strategies that were in the form of graphic organizers. Her plan was to teach two different kinds of graphic organizers for notes, the Cornell method and a three-column strategy, and see which one worked best.

JASON'S STORY

Jason was observing a high school U.S. history class. Much class time was spent discussing primary sources including pictures, political cartoons, or news articles all from the same time period. The key information of the lesson was almost entirely presented and developed in the discussion of the primary sources presented by the teacher.

The classroom teacher, Mr. Hartsworth, fascinated students with his historical (and hilarious) stories, leading students in discussions and problem solving. Students were riveted to the teacher's presentation—so much so that at the end of the class, students had empty notebooks, because they were so involved with the discussion they failed to take notes on the important issues.

This key information from the discussion was not present in bullet points on the board but rather in what the teacher said and in the primary source itself. The students, however, failed to take notes during this period of discourse and in effect failed to record much of the lesson's key information. This problem was best exemplified during one particular observation when the teacher was absent.

On that day the students were tasked with writing an in-class essay due at the end of the period. The students were required to support their arguments using specific examples from the primary source they discussed. Only six students or 20 percent of the class ever consulted their notes for this assignment. Instead, most of the class consulted textbooks, while a few neglected the assignment completely.

This clearly demonstrated a lack of notes on the primary sources and any key information uncovered in the class discussion among the majority of the class. Jason asked himself how these students could be aided to take better notes on this particular aspect of the classroom discourse. Jason decided to use a primary source analysis worksheet for students to take notes. (See figure 1.1.)

He predicted that while the primary source note-taking sheet might be met with some resistance, the sheet would provide a simple medium for students to take notes, ultimately increasing the amount of notes taken on a particular component under study.

DAILY CHALLENGES IN CLASSROOMS—
DESCRIBING THE PROBLEM

Danica and Jason are just two of the many new and nearly new teachers facing daily challenges in their classrooms. In addition to knowing content area and the pedagogy to teach content, teachers meet challenges with students, parents, colleagues, time management, classroom management, organizing materials—to name just a few. Even if teachers were to continuously take courses throughout their whole teaching career, they still would not have all the answers to all the challenges they would meet.

Danica and Jason, two students who were colleagues in the same teacher education program—who took all their pedagogy courses together—both faced situations involving note taking. Somewhere in their course of studies, they learned about note taking. Danica immediately knew about different forms of note taking—Cornell method, three-column strategy, and others. Jason recognized that if students did not

Primary Source Analysis Worksheet

Name: _____ Date: _____

Remember that a **Primary Source** is a source that comes directly from the time period under investigation. Answer the following questions about your source.

Type of Primary Source:

☐ Newspaper Article   ☐ Letter   ☐ Journal/Diary

☐ Cartoon/Comic   ☐ Audio Recording   ☐ Film Clip

☐ Photograph   ☐ Artifact   ☐ Map

☐ Poster/Advertisement   ☐ Government Document   ☐ Other: _____

Title of source: _____

Date of source: _____

Author/Creator of source: _____ Position/Title: _____

Audience source was created for: _____

List three things the author said (or that you notice) that you think are important:
1)
2)
3)

Why do you think this source was created?

What issues do you think are most important to the author/creator? Why?

What do you know now that the author/creator would have most liked to know?

Write a question to the author/creator of this source that is left unanswered:

Figure 1.1.   Indiana Historical Society Primary Source Analysis Worksheet

take notes even during discussions, they would have nothing to use as a basis for studying and understanding primary sources under review. Could they approach their problem—note taking—in the same way? After all, it was the same problem—or was it?

EXAMINING THE BACKGROUND
OF THOSE WITH THE PROBLEM

Although the problem might be considered as the same, every aspect that surrounded the note-taking problem contributed new information to how this problem needed to be considered and what kind of action plan could be a possible solution. When Danica and Jason met with their supervisor to discuss the problem, initially they were relieved to have the same problem. Simply put, students needed to take notes. That should be a quick and easy fix—tell them they have to take notes.

Jason and Danica brainstormed ideas after their initial visits to these classrooms to solve this problem. If students would take notes, they would have the materials they needed to respond to questions, write required essays, and participate in class discussions. What they discovered about their students led them in different directions for solving this problem.

Basically their students' problems were regarding note taking. However, the circumstances were very different. Danica's students had never been taught note taking. They lacked the skills needed to find and record important information and then to access the information they needed to respond to questions and essay prompts. Jason's students were in a different predicament. His students knew how to take notes from PowerPoint presentations and class lectures, but they could not transfer these same skills to note taking during discussions.

ACQUIRING KNOWLEDGE FROM RESEARCH

Recognizing these differences, Danica and Jason investigated what other educators did in similar situations. Danica found in the research that teaching students how to use Cornell notes not only supported note taking, but the notes also became a study guide (Fisher, Frey, & Williams, 2002). In another study she found that one note-taking strategy may be more beneficial than another, and that note-taking strategies may vary in usefulness by age level of the note taker (Risch & Kiewra, 1990). In yet another study she found that when students used graphic notes in contrast to linear notes, the notes were more beneficial for increasing text comprehension (Robinson, Katayama, Beth, Odom, Ya-Ping, & Vanderveen, 2006).

Jason found similar information regarding linear and nonlinear note taking. Students who take notes in a linear fashion rely on information presented in a linear format. And while there is "no difference in accuracy" between the two forms of note taking, nonlinear note takers were significantly better in quantity and quality of the learned material (Makany, Kemp, & Dror, 2009).

While that information was helpful, Jason realized that these students had already developed a linear form of note taking, and to switch their note-taking format at this late date in the school year might be problematic. In another study he found that when students took notes using guiding questions and with a set intention in mind—such as developing an argument—students profited from a nonlinear format. Thus, Jason introduced the primary source analysis worksheet (figure 1.1).

DEVISING A PLAN

Danica chose two note-taking strategies to teach her students. Both were in the form of a graphic organizer. On the first day she taught the Cornell method and implemented it with the reading of *The Kite Runner*. Students were given prompts to consider before they read the chapter. As they read the chapter, they took notes on the chapter by responding to the prompts. See figure 1.2.

On the second day, Danica taught the students the three-column strategy format for note taking (figure 1.3). Students were again given prompts to use while they independently read the chapter.

After students took notes using the prompts on each of the days, they participated in a teacher-led class discussion and were able to use their notes for reference during the discussion. Students also wrote a brief re-

Student Notes	*Student Conclusions*	
Throughout the chapter, Amir ignores Hassan	➔	Because of his guilt, Amir can't look at him the same way.
Baba and Amir's relationship improves	➔	It is improved ever since Amir's win at the kite tournament. The more he interacts with Baba the more he distances himself away from Hassan
Amir wanted new servants	➔	Baba quickly yelled at Amir for saying that he wanted new servants, considering that Ali and Baba are good friends.

Figure 1.2.   Student Work Sample (The Cornell Method)

Question	Answer	Symbol/Example
1) Why is the kite tournament so important?	It is a part of their culture	
2) Why doesn't Amir want to eat? (p. 81)	He can't stop thinking about Hassan	
3) Why is Amir not concerned about Hassan, and thinks Baba is ruining it when he mentions Hassan? (p. 82)	He wants Baba to himself	
4) Why did Amir lie to Ali?	He's scared to tell him about the rape	He avoided the question, and then got defensive when Ali asked again

Figure 1.3. Student Work Sample 1 (Three Column Strategy)

flection on the note-taking strategy they used indicating the usefulness of the strategy and whether they would use the strategy again.

Jason introduced his students to the primary source analysis worksheet (figure 1.1). This note-taking sheet was designed specifically for taking notes on primary sources. Students recorded information on the type of source, title of the source, date of creation, author of the source, and the audience of the source. The sheet also contained evaluative questions that prompted the students to stake a claim and defend it with support. In this way students sought to make an argument on the source and defend it. Each day students were given a new sheet for the primary source document they were discussing.

RESULTS OF THE PLAN

While Danica found that students were initially reluctant to break out of their habits of not taking notes, with her encouragement students began to take notes while they read. She noted a tremendous improvement in the students. Reading became more fun because they were engaged in the text through their notes. Their notes also helped them comprehend the text fully, which caused the class discussions to improve immensely. Students were participating and offering ideas and interpretations. The prompt was fully answered, and students seemed more confident in themselves.

Jason had a similar hypothesis regarding student note taking. The predicted outcome of this study was that, while the primary source note-taking sheets might be met with some resistance, they would ultimately provide a simple medium for students to take notes, thus increasing the amount of notes taken on the primary source document and the discussion about the document.

Using statistical information, Jason found that the primary source note-taking sheet did meet resistance as expected. At least 6.67 percent of the class completely rejected it. Another 33 percent of the class put minimal effort into the note-taking sheet or rushed through it, showing only some rejection. Also as predicted, the note-taking sheets provided an easy medium for students to take notes on the classroom discourse surrounding primary sources. Ultimately this sheet increased the amount of note taking that took place on the classroom discourse. This was noted because 93 percent of the students in the class had some form of notes on these primary sources. See figure 1.4.

	Group 1	*Group 2*	*Group 3*	*Group 4*
Completion rate:	0–25%	50%	75%	100%
Number of students:	2	10	16	2
Percent of class:	6.67%	33.33%	53.33%	6.67%

Figure 1.4.   Note completers using Primary Source Note taking Sheet

Assuming that the 20 percent in the observation during the teacher's absence is representative of the students who had notes on the primary sources, this would be an increase of 73.33 percent. The fact of the matter is that most students had not been taking any notes on the discourse surrounding primary sources, and with the implementation of this note-taking sheet, most students now had at least something on the primary sources.

Jason concluded that this primary source note-taking sheet increased the class's note taking on classroom discourse because the sheet provided an easy format to take notes, and in a way, required them to take notes on something they previously either chose not to take notes on or were unaware of how to take notes on. (See figure 1.1.)

WHAT THESE STUDENTS LEARNED

Danica reported several lessons she learned in the process of this action research. She listed the learning from two aspects—learning about teaching note taking and learning the value of action research.

Danica commented that a great surprise for her in this experience was the realization that these students were never taught note taking. "I spent eight weeks with these students during student teaching, and not once did I realize that the reason they didn't take notes was because they did not know how to take notes." Only after the student teaching experience, when she returned to do field hours, did she realize these students did not know how to take notes. Her research on the various forms of note taking and her learning in her classes helped her select two graphically organized formats for note taking which matched the needs for these students.

Through her observations and review of students' work, she learned that as students are learning note-taking strategies, they also need extensive practice in the process and continued feedback and support from the teacher. She learned that without a consistent use of note taking as part of course requirements, students very easily slip back into habits they cultivated in middle and high school classes where they took minimal or no notes.

Not only did Danica learn more about aspects of teaching and requiring note taking for her students in English class, but she also discovered the importance of action research for teachers. While doing her own research on note taking in the secondary classroom, she discovered that not only was there limited research at the secondary level, but also the research that was available was generally conducted by persons other than the classroom teacher. Most research was conducted by college professors, theorists, or statisticians studying teachers.

Another finding for Danica as a secondary major with a concentration in English was that action research was very different from the research that she did in her English courses. Most of her required English courses concentrated on literature, and the few courses that included a research component focused on literary studies and examining texts along the lines of a specific inquiry around a theme or topic and resulting in a thesis. As is the case with undergraduate research in the humanities

the products of research are predominantly intellectual and intangible, with the results contributing to an academic discipline and also informing other disciplines, a process which often effects individual or social change over time. In the humanities, this might consist of literary authorship, which creates new knowledge in the form of art, or scholarly research, which adds new knowledge by examining texts and other cultural artifacts in the pursuit of particular lines of scholarly inquiry. (University of Washington, 2015)

The contrast between the intellectual and intangible product of a paper in English and taking a specific course of action to change human behavior in education was mind-boggling. While her students were better off as learners from the note-taking strategies she taught them, she was far better prepared to address learning challenges knowing how to conduct action research.

Jason had a similar experience. One lesson for him that was reinforced by this experience was the constant process of developing as a teacher. He described teaching as a fluid process that evolves over the years. He concluded that a teacher should not teach the same way to every class every year.

Teachers must continue to develop their skills and incorporate new teaching styles and tools. Jason recognized the need for teachers to think constantly about how they can improve their teaching styles to meet each individual student learning style. Action research helped to reinforce these ideals in his mind. He acknowledged the benefits of action research to the teacher, the students, and the educational community as a whole.

A key skill gained from this experience was the ability to conduct action research. Teachers are always looking for better ways to teach students. They experiment and try new things all the time. When they find something that works, they run with it, but too often that is the end of the story. In his field experience Jason gained the skills to conduct research in the classroom in a way that is scientific. He acquired the skills necessary to create formal evaluations of data that can be examined by other teachers and possibly used in their own classrooms.

Jason concluded his reflection on his learning by stating:

> With knowledge gained from my observations and research, I feel I will better be able to help my students. I will be able to develop new ways of teaching that can address student struggles in the classroom. I believe action research will help me create a better classroom environment for the students. If the research is done in a way where it can be shared with other members of the educational community, this too will benefit students. It is possible that the action research of just one teacher could benefit the education of many different students in many different schools. (personal communication)

THE IMPACT OF ACTION RESEARCH IN TODAY'S CLASSROOMS AND ON TODAY'S STUDENTS

Teachers are expected to understand, study, and improve their classrooms. However, many reach the classroom without knowing and doing active, applied research on the following:

1. Understanding curriculum and what works or doesn't work
2. Helping children of various ages to learn and test well
3. Knowing best practices in classroom and student management and how to study these tasks
4. Selecting best strategies for improving instruction and learning
5. Giving examples that are real and that work for teachers on the job
6. Understanding and learning to manage the processes, requirements, and outcomes of school teaching
7. Understanding and being aware of the future of teaching and school improvement

Action research is the research of teachers, while research in general has many aims and outcomes. Research is generally characterized by an evidence-based question or hypothesis that is important to the discipline in which the research is conducted and follows a discipline-specific process. "Students, then, must know something about the research methodology of a discipline (what constitutes 'evidence' and how to obtain it) and how to decide if a question or line of inquiry that is interesting to that student is also important to the discipline, to be able to embark on a research project" (University of Washington, 2015).

Research in the humanities is very different from research in education. Humanities research results contribute to an academic discipline (English, social studies) and generally *effects individual or social change* over time. Action research is more immediate and impacts human performance.

Historically, educational research was done by professors, universities, and theorists on children, teachers, and the community. Action research is done by teachers. They participate in their own inquiry as both teacher and researcher. The primary focus of action research is to enhance the lives of students, develop professional dispositions, and reflect on practice (Mills, 2014).

Practice of one's teaching profession requires more than just knowing the content. Unlike taking a research course which results in a quantitative and/or qualitative research report, action research involves teachers in making change happen. The changes that are noted are in student learning and teacher teaching.

Teachers engage in a systematic study of a specific problem in a specific setting. Teachers systematically study what others have done in similar situations and use those findings to devise a plan of action to address the identified problem. They then study the results of student learning based on the implementation of the plan, make needed adjustments to the plan to promote even greater learning, and share the findings with other colleagues.

INCORPORATING RESEARCH FOR UNDERGRADUATES

Before teachers enter their own classrooms, they need experience with using action research. Once they have their own class, they need guidance in implementing action research. Many colleges are now including research experiences for students in all disciplines. The goal of the research is to actively engage students in contested questions based on observations in real settings and generate a sense of excitement as they pursue answers and solutions to the problems they observe and experience.

Kuh (2008) asserts that undergraduate research has been highly beneficial for undergraduate students, and thus undergraduate research is among the high-impact educational practices. The research indicates that students who have access to these high-impact educational practices have higher retention rates and student engagement.

Action research for undergraduate teacher candidates and teachers in actual classrooms serves two purposes: improve student learning—which is the ultimate goal of education—and improve the craft of teaching through reflective practice. Danielson's Framework for Teaching highlights this in Domain 4—Professional Responsibilities. She introduces Domain 4a—Reflecting on Teaching—with this description:

> Reflecting on teaching encompasses the teacher's thinking that follows any instructional event, an analysis of the many decisions made in both the planning and the implementation of a lesson. By considering these elements in light of the impact they had on student learning, teachers can determine where to focus their efforts in making revisions and choose which aspects of the instruction they will continue in future lessons. Teachers may reflect on their practice through collegial conversations, journal writing, examining student work, conversations with students, or simply thinking about their teaching. Reflecting with accuracy and specificity, as well as being able to use in future teaching what has been learned, is an acquired skill; mentors, coaches, and supervisors can help teachers acquire and develop the skill of reflecting on teaching through supportive and deep questioning. Over time, this way of thinking both reflectively and self-critically and of analyzing instruction through the lens of student learning—whether excellent, adequate, or inadequate—becomes a habit of mind, leading to improvement in teaching and learning. (Danielson, 2014, p. 83)

Teachers who incorporate thinking that is reflective and self-critical for analyzing student learning and their own teaching can use action research to develop this way of thinking. Reflective teachers and teacher researchers professionally invite themselves as well as others to be successful and cultivate an inviting attitude within and beyond school. One way to achieve this goal is to undertake a reflective approach to one's educational activities and to share the findings of these activities with others (Smith, 2010). Action research supports teachers in this endeavor.

As far back as 1926 the educational researcher B. R. Buckingham (1926) supported this idea when he stated: "The teacher has opportunities for research, which if seized, will not only powerfully and rapidly develop the technique of teaching, but will also react to vitalize and dignify the work of the individual teacher" (p. iv). Teachers have always been researchers. They learn best when they investigate their own practice and processes. This book is intended to assist teacher researchers in developing this craft and practice.

REFERENCES

Buckingham, B. R. (1926). *Research for teachers.* New York: Silver Burdett & Co.

Danielson, C. (2014). *The framework for teaching evaluation instrument,* 2013 edition. Princeton, NJ: The Danielson Group. Retrieved at www.danielsongroup.org.

Ferrance, E. (2000). *Themes in education: Action research.* The Education Alliance: Brown University, Providence, RI.

Fisher, D., Frey, N., & Williams, D. (2002). Seven literacy strategies that work. *Educational Leadership,* 70–73.

J. Foy, Personal communication, May 5, 2015.

Kuh, G. D. (2008). High-impact educational practices: What they are, who has access to them, and why they matter. Retrieved at https://www.aacu.org/leap/hips.

Makany, T., Kemp, J., & Dror, I. E. (2009). Optimising the use of note taking as an external cognitive aid for increasing learning. *British Journal of Educational Technology, 40,* 619–35. doi: 10.1111/j.1467-8535.2008.00906.x

Mills, G. E. (2014). *Action research: A guide for the teacher researcher* (5th ed.). New York: Pearson.

Risch, N. L., & Kiewra, K. A. (1990). Content and form variations in note taking: Effects among junior high students. *Journal of Educational Research, 83*(6), 355–57.

Robinson, D. H., Katayama, A. D., Beth, A., Odom, S., Ya-Ping, H., & Vanderveen, A. (2006). Increasing text comprehension and graphic note taking using a partial graphic organizer. *Journal of Educational Research, 100*(2), 103–11.

Smith, K. H. (2010). The inviting professional educator: A reflective practitioner and action researcher. *Journal of Invitational Theory and Practice, 16,* 5–9.

University of Washington undergraduate research program. (2015). Seattle: University of Washington. Retrieved at https://depts.washington.edu/engl/ugrad/researchtext.php.

2

✛

Understanding Teachers and Improving Life in the Classroom

What does action research show us about quality and improvement of classroom teaching and teachers' lives? How are life and professional improvement done? What roles do "professionalism" and "being perceived as a professional" play in training, nurturing, and improving teachers and teaching? The notion of teacher professionalism is either used or ignored in efforts to train and improve teachers' classroom instruction. And why is understanding teachers and teaching *in the classroom* so critical?

This chapter explains the roles and responsibilities of teachers, based on the development of the role as a "profession"—or what some have considered "teaching as a semiprofession." Teachers are considered "semiprofessionals" because unlike medical doctors or lawyers who can save people's lives after long training and interning, and are deemed full professionals governed by their association, such as the American Medical Association (AMA) and American Bar Association (ABA), teachers just teach. They merely lay the foundation for every professional.

BACKGROUND

Teaching is among the oldest "professions," jobs, and role models for children in the world, as schools have existed for centuries—and are not going away anytime soon. Yet for several reasons, teachers and their positions and roles have not been fully examined, understood, or improved upon over the last three decades or so. This chapter uses a long tradition of research to trace different views of *professionalism in education,* which along with other traditional "female jobs" (such as social work and nursing), has long been deemed semiprofessional.

As such, teaching is not considered a true "profession," as are the roles of doctors and lawyers, whose work often has a direct effect in real human life (and death) situations in medical operating rooms and courtrooms. And gender has long been a determinant of professional standing and research. For remember that "men make money while women just work hard," as the saying goes.

One male teacher experienced the following when trying to raise a family on a teacher's salary:

> Richie Brown, a North Carolina educator who was a candidate for teacher of the year, is the type of teacher whom every principal should want. He was teaching in a high-demand subject area in a low-income school just outside of Wilmington, North Carolina. However, Brown decided to *leave the profession* last year after six years of teaching, and the reason was simple: he did not earn enough money to support his family. (Boser & Straus, 2014, p. 4)

In the 1960s, working with his mentor, Amitai Etzioni, on a book, *The Semi-Professions: Their Work and Organization* (1969), Daniel C. Lortie contributed the "teacher" chapters, showing what was lacking for teachers in their work that prevented them from being real professionals. Later, Lortie (1975) published his own (now-classic) book in the field, *Schoolteacher: A Sociological Inquiry,* which spells out the qualities of teaching and how the skills are understood, taught, and practiced by teachers, whether they are seen as professionals or just semiprofessionals.

Research by Talbert and McLaughlin (1994) analyzed teacher professionalism in local schools, based on the level of "collegial interactions" in local schools. They found in sixteen diverse high schools that all key departments, schools, and districts play a role in supporting or undermining the professionalism of teachers in the following ways: (1) a shared technical culture (shared knowledge and standards); (2) strong service ethic; and (3) professional commitment. The data suggest that professionalism evolves within active learning communities of teachers.

CHARACTERISTICS OF A PROFESSION

What is a profession? *Merriam-Webster's Dictionary* (2015) gives this definition of the word:

a. a calling requiring specialized knowledge and often long and intensive academic preparation

b. a principal calling, vocation, or employment
c. the whole body of persons engaged in a calling

Taking this meaning, one can apply this to teaching as a profession. Andy Rutledge (2011) in his *Design Professionalism* (http://designprofes sionalism.com/index.php) lists ten fundamental characteristics of professionalism as seen in figure 2.1.

As one reviews these ten characteristics, some certainly depict teaching as a profession: greater responsibility, accountability, specialized theoretical knowledge, institutional preparation, direct work relationships, and ethical constraints. However, one would question other characteristics, such as the extent of a teacher's control over and ultimate responsibility for the teacher's own work, choice of clients, and achieving employment and success based on merit. Rutledge concludes that in the absence of merit-based employment, issues of responsibility, accountability, and ethical constraints become irrelevant, negating any otherwise-professional characteristics.

Professionals do not select which characteristics they want to embody. Professionals embody them all. Despite the number of characteristics of a profession (some report seven characteristics, others twelve characteristics, some six), the reality is that for teaching to be considered a profession, teachers have to have a mindset about the profession. Teaching as a profession is about improving teacher practice and ultimately student learning.

APPLIED RESEARCH ON TEACHERS' ROLES AND QUALITY

Thus, a first area of research in this field is on the role, responsibilities, and quality of teachers as professionals. In fact, Amitai Etzioni (1969) has categorized teachers as "semi-professionals" along with nurses and social workers. This chapter works to refute the validity of this teacher label and provide guidance for making teachers more professional.

Unless the field can reclassify teaching as a profession—with all the qualities, prestige, and productivity of other professions—we are limited in our view, value, and support of teachers as quasi- or semiprofessionals, despite the noted importance of teachers (and learning) to our children, families, communities, and society. For as Joseph Shedd and Samuel Bacharach (1991) explained in *Tangled Hierarchies,* "Teachers need flexibility to adapt to the uncertain situations and unique needs they confront in their classrooms" (p. 1).

Five areas of research are critical to understanding and defining teaching and improving the field and role. Research on teachers and their

1. **Great responsibility**
   Professionals deal in matters of vital importance to their clients and are therefore entrusted with grave responsibilities and obligations. Given these inherent obligations, professional work typically involves circumstances where carelessness, inadequate skill, or breach of ethics would be significantly damaging to the client and/or his fortunes.

2. **Accountability**
   Professionals hold themselves ultimately accountable for the quality of their work with the client. The profession may or may not have mechanisms in place to reinforce and ensure adherence to this principle among its members. If not, the individual professional will (e.g. guarantees and/or contractual provisions).

3. **Based on specialized, theoretical knowledge**
   Professionals render specialized services based on theory, knowledge, and skills that are most often peculiar to their profession and generally beyond the understanding and/or capability of those outside of the profession . . .

4. **Institutional preparation**
   Professions typically require a significant period of hands-on, practical experience in the protected company of senior members before aspirants are recognized as professionals. After this provisional period, ongoing education toward professional development is compulsory . . .

5. **Autonomy**
   Professionals have control over and, correspondingly, ultimate responsibility for their own work. Professionals tend to define the terms, processes, and conditions of work to be performed for clients (either directly or as preconditions for their ongoing agency employment).

6. **Clients rather than customers**
   Members of a profession exercise discrimination in choosing clients rather than simply accepting any interested party as a customer (as merchants do).

7. **Direct working relationships**
   Professionals habitually work directly with their clients rather than through intermediaries or proxies.

8. **Ethical constraints**
   Due to the other characteristics on this list, there is a clear requirement for ethical constraints in the professions. Professionals are bound to a code of conduct or ethics specific to the distinct profession (and sometimes the individual). Professionals also aspire toward a general body of core values, which are centered upon an uncompromising and unconflicted regard for the client's benefit and best interests.

9. **Merit-based**
   In a profession, members achieve employment and success based on merit and corresponding voluntary relationships rather than on corrupted ideals such as social principle, mandated support, or extortion (e.g. union members are not professionals). Therefore, a professional is one who must attract clients and profits due to the merits of his work. In the absence of this characteristic, issues of responsibility, accountability, and ethical constraints become irrelevant, negating any otherwise-professional characteristics.

10. **Capitalist morality**
    The responsibilities inherent to the practice of a profession are impossible to rationally maintain without a moral foundation that flows from a recognition of the singular right of the individual to his own life, along with all of its inherent and potential sovereign value; a concept that only capitalism recognizes, upholds and protects. (Rutledge, 2011. Section 1.1).

Figure 2.1. Andy Rutledge's Ten Characteristics of Professionalism
Reprinted with permission by the author.

status points the way toward understanding both the role of teachers and how to improve their standing and performance. Here are the issues and bodies of research to assist us: (1) access to the profession of teaching; (2) nature of the work; (3) delayed impact of teaching on children and society; (4) complexity of process of teaching; and (5) determining the quality of outcomes for students in school and life.

ACCESS TO THE PROFESSION OF TEACHING

Among the professions, teaching is much more accessible, open, and easy to enter. In fact, many colleges and universities enable their students to become licensed, certified teachers while completing their bachelor's degrees (BA or BS). While getting into a medical or law school—not to mention dentistry, business, or engineering—can be a difficult, demanding effort, one can "become a teacher" more easily and readily. Thus, research indicates that teaching is perhaps too easily entered and should be tightened up with higher standards. As OECD reported (2005):

> All across the globe, countries are trying to improve education. Some countries are in the earlier stages of education development, mainly striving to expand access to elementary and lower secondary education and to ensure transmission of basic skills; in these nations, reformers are less concerned with the quality of the teaching force than with just getting enough teachers into classrooms. Other countries are entering the global knowledge economy and seeking to prepare their students with the complex, higher-order cognitive skills that economy demands; in these nations, the major focus is strengthening the quality and effectiveness of the teacher workforce. (Organisation for Economic Cooperation and Development, 2005, p. 3)

Thus, research worldwide indicates the importance of teacher training and support to help nations to thrive; we also know that teachers together help shape and even create the next generations. So we too advocate that the United States focus on attracting, preparing, and supporting topnotch candidates to become teachers. Priorities matter, and so do great new generations of teachers for our children.

Other countries realize the importance of finding and supporting new teachers as their nations work to improve learning, work, income, and the economy. England, for example, has taken steps to raise the status of the profession through a sophisticated advertising campaign that recruited new candidates; a televised teacher awards programs; encouragement of alternate routes into teaching to compete with traditional university teacher training programs; and bonuses for those who commit to teach in high-need communities. As a result of these actions, teaching went from the ninety-second career choice to the top career choice within five years (Barber & Mourshed, 2007).

When shortages occur, all these countries focus on recruiting teachers in innovative ways, rather than lowering the standards to get more teachers. One added benefit of this attention to recruitment and induction is far lower attrition rates among new teachers than in the United States.

We acknowledge that the United States concentrates on local and state education personnel policies, and thus, a national teacher training effort will be more difficult. But certainly the national leadership can press and finance programs that are (a) more extensive, (b) more available, (c) of higher quality, and (d) available to all people who are interested in becoming teachers.

QUALITY AND NATURE OF THE WORK IN SCHOOL

Once quality teachers are recruited, trained, and employed in our schools, how do we keep them and nourish them in their teaching? Clearly, the ability of schools and communities to find and keep good teachers, if not the best, is the next problem.

What does the action research tell us about nurturing and keeping teachers in their work? Harry K. Wong (2004) explains about teachers that "their success will determine the success of an entire generation of students. Their success can be ensured by providing them with a comprehensive, coherent professional development program" (p. 41). Wong suggests that teacher mentoring is a component of an induction program which is a component of professional development. New and nearly new teachers need all three components.

Mentoring is a critical support to new teachers. However,

Feiman-Nemser (1996) found that after reviewing 20 years of claims about mentoring, few studies existed that showed the context, content, and consequences of mentoring. Serpell and Bozeman (1999) reported on beginning teacher induction and stated that the mentoring component is essential to many induction programs, but it is not helpful in and of itself. Schlager, Fusco, Koch, Crawford, and Phillips (2003) stated that new teachers' needs are so varied and immediate that the appropriate combination of expertise, experience, and cultural background is unlikely to reside in one mentor who is available when needed. Lehman (2003) wrote that every district should offer a multi-year induction program that provides systematic help and support, and this cannot be done adequately by another teacher with a full-time load who drops by when time permits or when a problem arises. (Wong, 2004, p. 44)

Thus, Wong concludes that leadership is critical to supporting, improving, and keeping good teachers; mentoring alone is not enough. An induction program is not enough. Planned and purposeful professional development, individually crafted for each teacher, promotes quality within the teacher and thus enhances the whole school community. As Wong states:

> Successful teachers, especially in hard-to-staff schools, must have strong leaders. Good teachers do not choose to remain at schools where principals perform poorly. Effective leadership means involving teachers in key instructional decisions and providing opportunities for teachers to learn from each other. Good teachers know that they must have colleagues who have similar standards and expectations. Accomplished teachers are more likely to choose to work in schools when there will be a "critical mass" of like-minded colleagues who share their commitment to student achievement and where the principal is the key to establishing this commitment to teacher improvement and student achievement. The bottom line is good teachers make the difference. Trained teachers are effective teachers. Districts that provide structured, sustained training for their teachers achieve what every school district seeks to achieve—improving student learning. (Wong, 2004, p. 55)

As we look to the effects of good teachers on student performance, the results are striking. When and if students have a succession of outstanding teachers, data support the assertion that having an effective teacher instead of an average teacher for four or five years in a row could essentially close the gap in math performance between students from low-income and high-income households (Hanushek, Kain, & Rivkin, 2001). Sanders and Rivers (1996) concluded that children who had the most effective teachers three years in a row posted academic achievement gains that were 54 percent higher than children who had the least effective teachers three years in a row.

One other essential component for new teachers is knowing how well they are doing. Receiving feedback on performance can help teachers continuously grow and improve. Phillips (2013), through her work at the Bill and Melinda Gates Foundation, reports:

> Teachers have always wanted better feedback, and the MET project has highlighted tools like student surveys and observations that can allow teachers to take control of their own development. The combination of those measures and student growth data creates actionable information that teachers can trust. (2013)

Thus, we can see that research shows the effects of good teaching on students and their learning and achievement. The problems with making this happen are several: (1) Do we really know what good teachers look like and do? (2) How do we measure it in ways other than measuring *student progress*? (3) Can we control which students get which teachers, and what effect would that have on student programs? and (4) Do we know which teachers are best to teach children of different backgrounds, needs, skills, and intelligence? The answer to all of these questions is "No!"

The relationships between particular teachers and each student are simply so complex and difficult that we cannot come up with one formula for assessing teachers and their effects and effectiveness on individual students—not to mention on other teachers and colleagues. Teachers need to develop as the professionals and practitioners who provide the answers to these questions. Becoming teacher researchers will allow teachers to find answers to the myriad of questions and challenges they will face in their classrooms.

DELAY OF TEACHING RESULTS AND REWARDS

Another difficulty that teachers often face is the slowness and obscurity of job and career outcomes. On one microlevel, teachers each have to wait until their students are taught something, tested on it, and averaged over time. It might take a whole grading period to see how the ranges of students do with their teacher. And on a macrolevel, it takes nearly a lifetime to discover how students are doing in college, training, jobs, and careers—and their lives.

Teacher thus often get "results" that are long-term, delayed, and confusing. A poor student in one teacher's class may grade and average low in that teacher's subject but do well in life; while sometimes the bright wiz kids fail to get practical training, advanced degrees, and good jobs that can lead to strong, high lifetime earning and prestigious spending. Thus, we as teachers remember those moments when a former student compliments us on our techniques.

I remember teaching a class five new vocabulary words daily; over a year later, one student called to thank me for preparing her for College Board and other standardized tests that require a strong vocabulary. I glowed for days, since feedback is so long-term, vague, and nonexistent that teachers may work for forty years and never really know how their lessons and activities may have benefited their students—or not.

When I retired after nearly fifty years of teaching at the University of Pennsylvania, Dartmouth College, and Fordham University in New York City, my wife held a dinner retirement party at Fordham University, and 140 former graduate students, many of whom I had mentored to their doctorates, attended. I was shocked, moved, and thankful for recognition at retirement of a career of teaching educational teachers and leaders.

Thus, immediate and long-term (lifetime) assessment of teachers lacks good feedback, rewards, and sanctions after breaking into the field. While lawyers, doctors, and business people get feedback in their salaries and prestige fairly quickly and consistently (if not yearly), teachers are paid much lower salaries and receive few benefits of their successes. Merit-based employment does not exist for U.S. classrooms, accomplishments, and their teachers.

COMPLEXITY OF THE TEACHING PROCESS

Teaching is a complex process. Sagor (2000) describes the choice to be a teacher in this way:

> For people who don't enjoy a challenge, choosing to become a teacher is the worst possible career decision. Nothing in the schoolhouse works easily or smoothly. In fact, few if any schools can claim to perform as consistently as NASA's space shuttle. This isn't because the space shuttle is a simple machine—which it isn't—but because success in education, like all other human endeavors, is influenced by an infinite array of variables. (p. 36)

Teaching is an art and a science, and the effective teacher is both artist and scientist. What makes the process so complex? In considering innate talent, people are often classified as either a artist or a scientist. Teachers have to be both.

Consider the role of the fourth-grade teacher in helping students understand and use long division or fractions, or even consider the counties in the state in a social studies lesson. How hard can that be? Most of us can still remember the steps in performing long division. That's the science of long division. How many of us can come up with ways to entice fourth-graders to learn these steps and then apply long division to real-life situations? That's the artistry required in this simple lesson.

Far beyond planning the lesson is the consideration of the twenty-five fourth-graders who will be taught the lesson. Each child is at a unique level of learning. Each child is different, with varying backgrounds, interests, and social and emotional needs. All of these variables need to be considered as that teacher attempts to help pupils learn long division.

The perfect school day, when the sun is shining just right; the temperature inside and out is just perfect; all supplies and materials are right where they need to be; the Smart Board is working just fine; and there have been no interruptions from the office, another classroom, or within the classroom (perhaps one in 180 days of the school year) is the day teaching is less complex. That is the day when designing the space shuttle is more complicated than teaching. Don't be absent on that day . . . you will have missed the single opportunity of the school year to see teaching in its "noncomplex" format.

DETERMINING THE QUALITY OF OUTCOMES FOR STUDENTS IN SCHOOL AND LIFE

The connection between quality teaching and student achievement is one topic that has captured the attention of many policy makers and practitioners. The purpose of schools is student learning. Teachers have the greatest impact on student learning. As stated above, it may be years before teachers know the impact they had on students.

Teachers cannot wait years to determine the quality of their practice. Each year in a student's life, the student is impacted by the teacher in the classroom. Haim Ginnot (1972) stated that reality this way:

> I have come to the frightening conclusion that I am the decisive element. It is my personal approach that creates the climate. It is my daily mood that makes the weather. I possess tremendous power to make life miserable or joyous. I can be a tool of torture or an instrument of inspiration; I can humiliate or humor, hurt or heal. In all situations, it is my response that decides whether a crisis is escalated or de-escalated, and a person is humanized or de-humanized.

The quality of outcomes for students can be determined by the day-to-day interactions between teachers and students. While the long-lasting effects of the educational outcomes may be harder to assess, the impact of the teacher on a student is easier to determine.

Much research has been done on the psychosocial characteristics of elementary and secondary school environments. The classroom environment is an active field of study and a critical component for determining teacher effectiveness.

Danielson (2013) includes classroom environment as one of the four domains in her teaching framework. Included in this domain are (1) creating an environment of respect and rapport; (2) establishing a culture for learning; (3) managing classroom procedures; (4) managing student behavior; and (5) organizing physical space. Danielson explains in each component of the classroom environment domain how the highly effective teacher impacts the outcomes for students by the way the teacher responds in the classroom and beyond the classroom.

Taylor (2009) developed a theory regarding the relationship between environment and design within the classroom. They referred to the physical environment of the classroom as the "silent curriculum" and hold strongly to the belief that understanding the physical environment is essential to the education of children. Their research asserts that the teacher must know the environment and act responsibly within the environment. Their research as well as the research across other academic disciplines indicates that the classroom environment affects student behavior, academic achievement, and overall student development.

What students experience and learn in the classroom will impact them for life. Students decide every day which classrooms they want to enter and stay in. The most decisive element in that classroom is the teacher who creates the environment.

OVERCOMING PROBLEMS USING ACTION RESEARCH

As this book demonstrates, the issues and problems confronting our teachers are only partially overcome by research; teachers, particularly newer (untenured) teachers, need to understand both the importance and limitations of being a teacher and how to use the important role in their lives and careers. It will not come easily or quickly, but good teachers find out over their lifetime just how important, rewarding, and meaningful teaching is and can be over their lifetime and beyond.

Research has struggled to find the key to unlock the way to train, support, and reward teachers and their effectiveness. Many people emphasize the importance of good teachers, and many local, state, and federal policies are designed to promote teacher quality. Research using student scores on standardized tests confirms the common perception that some teachers are more effective than others and also reveals that being taught by an effective teacher has important consequences for student achievement.

The Rand Corporation (2014) came up with several principles that are based on applied action research. See figure 2.2.

Teachers will choose their level of professionalism by their actions. Rutledge's (2011) first two characteristics of professionalism—*great responsibility* and *accountability*—will help new and nearly new, as well as veteran teachers, to understand their own roles and how they are responsible for improving life in the classroom. They take responsibility for their actions and they hold themselves accountable for the quality of their work with their students. This is the work of the professional, this is the mission of the teacher, and this is the value of action research in the classroom.

- *Teachers matter more to student achievement than any other aspect of schooling.* Many factors contribute to a student's academic performance, including individual characteristics and family and neighborhood experiences. But research suggests that, among school-related factors, teachers matter most. When it comes to student performance on reading and math tests, a teacher is estimated to have two to three times the impact of any other school factor, including services, facilities, and even leadership.
- *Nonschool factors do influence students' achievement, but they are largely outside of school's control.* Some research suggests that, compared with teachers, individual and family characteristics may have four to eight times the impact on student achievement. But policy discussions focus on teachers because it is arguably easier for public policy to improve teaching than to change students' personal characteristics or family circumstances. Effective teaching has the potential to help level the playing field.
- *Effective teachers are best identified by their performance, not by their background or experience.* Despite common perceptions, effective teachers cannot reliably be identified based on where they went to school, whether they're licensed, or (after the first few years) how long they've taught. The best way to assess teachers' effectiveness is to look at their on-the-job performance, including what they do in the classroom and how much progress their students make on achievement tests. This has led to more policies that require evaluating teachers' on-the-job performance, based in part on evidence about their students' learning.
- *Effective teachers tend to stay effective even when they change schools,* as recent evidence suggests that a teacher's impact on student achievement remains reasonably consistent even if the teacher changes schools and regardless of whether the new school is more or less advantaged than the old one.

Figure 2.2.   Rand Corporation Principles on Action Research

REFERENCES

Barber, M., & Mourshed, M. (2007). *How the world's best-performing school systems come out on top.* London: McKinsey and Company.

Boser, U., & Straus, C. (2014, July 23). *Mid- and late-career teachers. Struggle with paltry incomes.* Center for American Progress.

Danielson, C. (2013). *Framework for teaching evaluation instrument.* Princeton, NJ: The Danielson Group.

Etzioni, A. (Ed.) (1969). *The semi-professions: Their work and organization.* New York: Macmillan.

Feiman-Nemser, S. (1996). *Teacher mentoring: A critical review.* Washington, DC: ERIC Clearinghouse on Teaching and Teacher Education. ERIC Document Reproduction Service No. ED397060.

Ginnot, H. G. (1972). *Teacher and child: A book for parents and teachers.* New York: Macmillan.

Hanushek, E. A., Kain, J. F., & Rivkin, S. G. (2001). *Why public schools lose teachers* (NBER Working Paper No. 8599). Cambridge, MA: National Bureau of Economic Research.

Lehman, P. (2003, November 26). Ten steps to school reform at bargain prices. *Education Week, 23*(13), 36, 28.

Lortie, D. C. (1975). *Schoolteacher: A sociological inquiry.* Chicago: University of Chicago Press.

Organisation for Economic Cooperation and Development. (2005). *Teachers matter: Attracting, developing and retaining effective teachers.* Paris: Author.

Phillips, V. (2013). *Findings help inform design and implementation of high-quality feedback and evaluation systems.* New York: Gates Foundation.

Profession. (n.d.). Retrieved June 2, 2015, from http://www.merriam-webster.com/dictionary/profession.

Rand Corporation. (2014). *Teachers matter: Understanding teachers' impact on student achievement.* nd.org/education/projects/measuring-teacher-effectiveness/teachers-matter.html.

Rutledge, A. (2011). *Design professionalism: The designers guide to taking back your profession.* Retrieved from http://designprofessionalism.com/index.php.

Sagor, R. (2000). *Guiding school improvement with action research.* Alexandria, VA: Association for Supervision and Curriculum Development.

Sanders, W. L., & Rivers, J. C. (1996). *Cumulative and residual effects of teachers on future student academic achievement.* Knoxville: University of Tennessee Value-Added Research and Assessment Center.

Schlager, M., Fusco, J., Koch, M., Crawford, V., & Phillips, M. (2003, July). *Designing equity and diversity into online strategies to support new teachers.* Paper presented at the National Educational Computing Conference (NECC), Seattle.

Serpell, Z., & Bozeman, L. (1999). *Beginning teacher induction: A report on beginning teacher effectiveness and retention.* Washington, DC: National Partnership for Excellence and Accountability in Teaching.

Shedd, J. B., & Bacharach, S. B. (1991). *Tangled hierarchies: Teachers as professionals and the management of schools.* Hoboken, NJ: Jossey-Bass.

Talbert, J. E., & McLaughlin, M. W. (1994). Teacher professionalism in a local context. *American Journal of Education, 102*(22), 244–257.

Taylor, A. (2009). *Linking architecture and education: Sustainable design for learning environments.* Albuquerque: University of New Mexico Press.

Wong, H. K. (2004, March). Induction programs that keep new teachers teaching and improving. *NASSP Bulletin, 88*(638), 41–58.

3

Principals' Role in Supporting Research and Improving Practices for New Teachers

How can both new and less-experienced teachers build action research into their classrooms—and thus improve their methods and outcomes with the help of their leaders? What help with—and support in—the process can effective principals and other school administrators provide for these teachers in using action research to improve student learning?

Based on useful applied research in the field, this chapter examines how effective principals can and do create a school environment that fosters quality and innovation in the classroom. Effective leadership can improve collegiality among staff, create a secure environment for teaching and learning, and promote an inquiry stance that (a) rewards teachers' efforts in trying new pedagogical methods and curricula, (b) improves teacher security and even tenure for new teachers, and (c) builds and reinforces new ideas for promoting student learning.

RELATIONSHIP BETWEEN TEACHERS AND ADMINISTRATORS

Relating to superiors in any job is a challenge—but this is especially true for the new and inexperienced. A first teaching position requires so many new applications, including relating to the "boss." Understanding their own new role as teachers is a new reality of stepping (literally) to "the other side of the desk."

The new teacher—especially the teacher who is just out of college and in a first postcollege workplace situation—has to find his or her place in this new environment. Up to this point in life, the new teacher has

associated with same-age colleagues—since preschool. The new workplace has not only a variety of personalities and backgrounds within the
faculty, but also the age differences are a new challenge for first-time
teachers. In addition to the challenge of developing collegial work relationships, the new teacher needs to develop the professional skills of
working with administrators.

While the key focus for teachers is student learning, the key focus for
administrators is teacher effectiveness. Effective administrators are available to teachers. Principals and those in administrative positions can only
know how well a teacher is doing by spending time with a teacher—
especially in a teacher's classroom.

Bonnie Grossen from the University of Oregon created an educator's
to-do list to assist administrators in low-performing schools. The list
included (1) visit every teacher's classroom every day; (2) focus on the
teacher's instructional delivery; (3) help teachers resolve conflicts in a
timely and efficient way; (4) support teachers in their disciplinary actions;
(5) be sure teachers have the materials they need; (6) minimize interruptions to teaching; and (7) teach a lesson with a new teacher (McEwan,
2003). Teachers will come to know and value the expertise of administrators as they spend time with them in educational experiences.

The Wallace Foundation (2011) identified several key functions of principal leadership that can shed light on issues confronting new teachers:

- Identifying problems confronted by new teachers
- Creating a climate hospitable to education where safety, a cooperative spirit, and other foundations of fruitful interaction prevail
- Cultivating leadership in others so that teachers and other adults assume their part in realizing the school vision
- Improving instructions to enable teachers to instruct at their best and
  thus have students learn at their utmost.

This chapter helps principals understand how they can assist new
teachers in trying action research in their classrooms without fear of being penalized by or degraded with evaluation reports. ERIC published
an important research paper by Marzano, Waters, and McNulty (2005)
called "School Leadership That Works: From Research to Results," done
by the Association for Supervision and Curriculum Development (ASCD)
that showed:

> What can school leaders really do to increase student achievement, and
> which leadership practices have the biggest impact on school effective-
> ness? . . . From 35 years of studies, the authors explain critical leadership

principles that every administrator needs to know: (1) The twenty-one leadership responsibilities that have a significant effect on student learning and the correlation of each responsibility to academic achievement gains; (2) The difference between first-order and second-order change and the leadership responsibilities—in rank order—that are most important for each; (3) How to choose the right work to focus on to improve student achievement; (4) The advantages and disadvantages of comprehensive school reform models for improving student achievement; (5) Eleven factors and thirty-nine actions that help you take a site-specific approach to improving student achievement; and (6) A five-step plan for effective school leadership that includes a strong team, distributed responsibilities, and thirty-one team action steps. (Marzano, Waters, & McNulty, 2005, p. 84)

UNDERSTANDING NEW TEACHERS' PROBLEMS

Much research has shown problems that new teachers find and confront in their classrooms and schools. For example, Carver (2003) noted:

> Research has found that large proportions of new teachers leave the profession within their first three to five years, just as they are getting their professional feet wet (Darling-Hammond, 1997). Many find the job impossible and the demands too great. Many new teachers leave the profession because of poor working conditions, including low pay and status. Others leave because of a lack of support from administrators, colleagues, students, and parents. (Ingersoll, 2001, p. 500)

Carver (2003) concludes that school principals must understand the needs of their teachers and find ways to help and value quality programs for new and perhaps all teachers. He wrote:

> To do this important work, principals must be knowledgeable about induction program goals and activities. They need to demonstrate an understanding of mentors' work with new teachers, including a healthy respect for mentor-novice confidentiality, and they need to become more aware of new teacher development and learning needs. School districts should provide meaningful professional development opportunities for principals that are focused on the effective practice of new teacher support, development, and assessment. (p. 44)

The focus of this chapter is thus on how those in leadership positions— e.g., principals, assistant principals, department chairs, and new teacher mentors— could and should help new teachers to try new things (e.g., action research) in their classrooms and thus become more effective teachers.

LEADERSHIP ROLES

"Leadership is second only to teaching among school influences on student success, and its impact is greatest in schools with the greatest need" (Wallace Foundation, 2013). Leaders at all levels in schools should perform the following five roles to guide schools to better teaching and learning: (1) shape and communicate a vision of academic success for all students; (2) create a climate hospitable to education; (3) cultivate leadership in others; (4) improve instruction; and (5) manage people, data, and processes to foster school improvement.

SHAPING A VISION OF ACADEMIC
SUCCESS FOR ALL STUDENTS

Beliefs and vision are crucial. For traditionally, the school principal was deemed "middle management," which is changing as individual schools become more critical, more responsible, and more often locally controlled—and school leadership resembles "top management" of the system in critical ways:

> Traditionally, the principal resembled the middle manager suggested in William Whyte's 1950's classic *The Organization Man*—an overseer of buses, boilers and books. Today, in a rapidly changing era of standards-based reform and accountability, a different conception has emerged—one closer to the model suggested by Jim Collins' *Good to Great* (2001), which draws lessons from contemporary corporate life to suggest leadership that focuses with great clarity on what is essential, what needs to be done and how to get it done. (Breidenstein, Fahey, Glickman, & Hensley, 2012, p. 11)

We know that the school leadership matters and that research shows that a clear vision and mission make huge differences in teachers' dedication, sense of support, and student outcomes. The so-called Wallace Perspective is useful here:

> Hasn't concern with the academic achievement of every student always topped principals' agendas? The short answer is, no. For years public school principals were seen as school managers, and as recently as two decades ago, high standards were thought to be the province of the college bound. "Success" could be defined as entry-level manufacturing work for students who had followed a "general track," and low-skilled employment for dropouts. Only in the last few decades has the emphasis shifted to academic expectations for all. (Wallace, 2013, p. 7)

A shared vision focused on learning for all students needs to be communicated in more than just words. Having a vision and communicating the vision are not the same thing. New teachers especially need to know and understand the vision administrators have for the school if these teachers are to share and support that vision.

Administrators can communicate a vision in many ways. Explicitly, administrators spell out the standards and goals for all learners. How administrators use their time and energies tells teachers what is valued in the school.

Some specific ways administrators—particularly principals—communicate what is important can be by sharing with teachers current research articles which can be discussed at faculty meetings. Teachers—especially those who are new—should be directed to visit exemplary models of instructional practices that the school is promoting. Observing highly qualified teachers can be a great lesson for new teachers and a way to recognize and acknowledge the accomplishments of veterans.

Administrators should use observation trends to plan professional development for teachers. They should continuously ask teachers how their decisions are impacting students. Administrators communicate their vision by the examples they exhibit in their own reflection on their practice and how that practice impacts the whole school community.

CREATING A CLIMATE HOSPITABLE TO EDUCATION

Once leadership is clearly focused, the next step is for everyone, as led by principals and other administrators (e.g., assistant principals, department chairs, and program coordinators), to make schools happy and focused places for students to learn—and for teachers to teach. As research shows, everyone needs to be part of the effort:

> A particularly noteworthy finding, reinforced in a major study by researchers at the University of Minnesota and University of Toronto, is the empirical link between school *leadership* and improved student *achievement*. Drawing on detailed case studies and large-scale quantitative analysis, the research shows that most school variables, considered separately, have at most small effects on learning. The real payoff comes when individual variables combine to reach critical mass. (Wallace, 2013, p. 5)

Effective principals and administrators assure that learning is at the center of what goes on in school every day and in every classroom. A climate hospitable to education is a healthy school environment that promotes safety and well-being, orderliness, and responsiveness, where children are valued and teachers feel they are part of a community of professionals who promote good instruction.

Trust begins with the principal. How the principal treats staff and students will result in how they treat each other. Principals needs to communicate fairness and eliminate fear. They need to respond calmly and with kindness. "Thank you" should be a common expression of gratitude and respect heard frequently and genuinely. The administrators need to be trustworthy—keeping promises made, valuing confidentiality, and communicating regularly—person to person as well as to the whole learning community.

Effective principals welcome and use feedback from all stakeholders. They listen, reflect, and then respond. They are transparent in how and why they make the choices and decisions they do and they are deliberate in sharing this information. What is valued by the principal becomes valued by the faculty and thus valued by the students.

In schools where student learning is valued, this is evident throughout the school. Student work decorates hallways; principals and administrators post notes on students' work; learning is obvious in the gym, the lunchroom, the principal's office, and when possible, even outside the school.

The principal is truly a learning leader who values the learning of students as well as the learning for staff. Questions and inquiry are rewarded. Teachers perform best in schools that provide a climate that focuses on learning for all. Principals and administrators can move from good to great as Collins (2001) suggests, following the hedgehog model of not doing many things well, but rather focusing with great clarity on the one or two things that the principal does better than anyone else—and doing it over and over again.

CULTIVATING LEADERSHIP IN OTHERS

Research also shows that leaders cannot lead alone, both as principals and as educators. (One finds no such thing as "leading alone.") Department chairs, for example, are there to help and inspire teachers and students in their grade-level and/or subject area, helping them to do great jobs—and to be able to turn to them if they need help. And teachers are, after all, *leaders in the classrooms*, giving ideas and direction to their pupils—thus exhibiting the qualities of good leaders in directing and inspiring their colleagues and students.

As Louis, Leithwood, Anderson, and Wahlstrom (2010) asked, why is leadership so crucial? One explanation they gave is that "leaders have the potential to unleash latent *capacities* in organizations . . . Principals and district leaders have the most influence on decisions in all schools; however, they do not lose influence as others gain influence" (p. 19).

Cultivating leadership promotes leadership. Effective administrators invite faculty and staff to lead learning. This is observed when teachers are asked to make presentations at faculty or parent meetings, when teachers are invited to consider ways to handle situations and provide insights, and when teachers are acknowledged for the success of their students or their own accomplishments.

Promoting leadership is not an alternative to dumping unwanted tasks on others. Administrators note the talents of their staff and celebrate these talents. Faculty meetings become the faculty's meeting, and principals and administrators are a part of the professional conversation that focuses on important issues for student learning and growth.

Personal goals are shared, and schoolwide goals are created by the whole faculty. Each contribution from a faculty member is recognized as a significant opportunity for student learning.

As the Wallace Foundation (2013) explained concerning leadership and the transformation of failing schools:

> Armed with what we've learned about the potential for leadership over the last decade, there is cause for optimism that the education community's long neglect of leadership is at last coming to an end. We still have a lot to learn, but we have already learned a great deal. In the face of this growing body of knowledge and experience, it is clear that now is the time to step up efforts to strengthen school leadership. Without effective principals, the national goal we've set of transforming failing schools will be next to impossible to achieve. (p. 17)

We can add that without cultivating leadership in others, our schools are doomed to fail.

IMPROVING INSTRUCTION

When leadership in a school communicates a vision of academic success for all students, creates a climate hospitable for education, and cultivates leadership among staff, improving instruction is a logical next step. Administrators cannot do it all.

In a report from the Wallace Foundation (2010) on effective leadership in high schools, some conditions were found that prevent principals from leading school improvement:

> In some districts, administrators attempt to exert complete control over every phase of instruction and school operations. They try to own all the

problems and enforce all solutions from the top down. In other districts, administrators turn all the problems over to the principal, offering little or no sense of direction or support—just a demand for results. Five of the seven districts studied fell into one of these two categories. In the two highly supportive districts, however, district and school board leaders exhibited a clear vision of what constitutes a good school and have created a framework in which the principal has autonomy to work with faculty on an improvement agenda with collaborative support from the district. Few principals have the capacity to rise above a school district's lack of vision and clear purpose. If district leaders cannot see beyond "test-prep"—if they expend most of the system's time, attention and energy on getting kids to pass low-level tests and meet minimum standards—then even the most capable principals will likely find themselves trapped in caretaker roles, presiding over schools and faculties that lack the direction, the goals and the belief in themselves necessary to create a powerful learning experience for all their students. (p. ii)

Principals, administrators, and teacher leaders must engage in designing instructional programs that result in all students prepared for life and work in the twenty-first century. These programs include relevant and rigorous learning experiences that involve students in hands-on learning activities and solving real-world problems. Programs must include critical and creative thinking, collaboration, and communication. Life skills of flexibility, initiative, productivity, leadership, and perseverance need to be taught and incorporated within the instructional program.

Decision making must be made at the school level and encouraged in each classroom setting. Teachers need autonomy in making decisions that best meet the needs of their students. This is not to suggest that teachers make decisions outside the realm of the school's vision, but teachers are encouraged and acknowledged for the steps they take in addressing needs of all students.

Principals need autonomy in selecting teachers that best meet the needs of students within their school. They need to make local decisions on scheduling, resources, and how best to align learning for students and work for teachers. They need to work within parameters of fiscal allotments and use fiscal responsibility for making instruction a priority.

MANAGING PEOPLE, DATA, AND PROCESSES

Overall, then, school leaders must balance their management of people with their data collection and analysis and improving the teaching and learning processes. It's a complex process, with principals concentrating on all three areas: (1) the *people* (e.g., teachers, kids, and parents); (2) the *data* (such as collecting and analyzing student attendance—and absenteeism—both in school [Shute & Cooper, 2014, 2015] and out of school, student grades, and improvements by subject and teacher); and (3) the *teaching-learning processes* in classes and schools, and by teachers.

Leaders for twenty-first-century schools lead with courage and conviction. They lead for the success of students and not for the comfort of adults. As one principal said, "I have my mantra about my leadership, and it is always the same question I pose to all who ask permissions, exceptions, and exemptions: *What is best for the students?* It is not about the adults—parents, teachers, staff—it is about the students. This is not always the question adults want to answer—but it is how I make decisions and invite others to make decisions." (personal communication)

Data can be a friend to principals and administrators. Data and knowledge can be used to make a difference in student learning and teacher teaching. The National Association of Elementary School Principals (2008) suggests that principals:

> make performance data a primary driver for school improvement; measure student, adult and school performance using a variety of data; build capacity of adults and students to use knowledge effectively to make decisions; benchmark high-achieving schools with comparable demographics; make results transparent to the entire school community. (p. 9)

Principals and administrators cannot base decisions only on a hunch or feeling. They use multiple measures of data over time, and they use teachers and students as a part of that data. Showing growth in student learning and examining processes teachers used in teaching support the data for what was done right and what still needs to be improved. And it is okay to still need to get better. This message should be what school is all about—we are all here to learn, and we learn constantly.

GOOD LEADERSHIP CAN IMPROVE STUDENT PERFORMANCE

Finally, we find that concerned principals, vice principals, and department or grade-level chairs—working closely and well with classroom teachers— can make a great difference in student learning and a school's quality and reputation. Obviously, new teachers require the most immediate and consistent help, although all teachers—even classroom veterans—can also benefit from some quality supervision, ideas, and help, to keep up in their fields and work. Leadership in schools is critical for everyone.

> The Vanderbilt Assessment of Leadership in Education, a tool to assess principal performance developed by researchers at Vanderbilt University, suggests that there are six key steps—or "processes"—that the effective principal takes when carrying out his or her most important leadership responsibilities: planning, implementing, supporting, advocating, communicating

and monitoring. The school leader pressing for high academic standards would, for example, map out rigorous targets for improvements in learning (planning), get the faculty on board to do what's necessary to meet those targets (implementing), encourage students and teachers in meeting the goals (supporting), challenge low expectations and low district funding for students with special needs (advocating), make sure families are aware of the learning goals (communicating), and keep on top of test results (monitoring). (Porter & Murphy et al., 2008, p. 22)

Neither teachers nor administrators have to go it alone. One approach is to see education in a wider and broader context, "from cradle-to-grave," as one major investment company with the federal government took the challenge:

> Goldman Sachs partners chose to support the Harlem Children's Zone (HCZ) through *Goldman Sachs Gives* because of its unique "cradle-to-college" approach. Funding for the school building was made possible, in part, by a $60 million grant from the New York City Department of Education's Charter Facilities Matching Grant Program, a $20 million gift from *Goldman Sachs Gives* and other private supporters.
>
> In addition, *Goldman Sachs Gives* convened the 21 communities that received grants under President Obama's Promise Neighborhoods initiative for a two-day Leadership Academy. The Promise Neighborhoods program is the national effort to replicate the success of the Harlem Children's Zone around the country. In conjunction with Harlem Children's Zone and Policy Link's Promise Neighborhood Institute, project managers, CEOs and school leaders received robust training around leadership, communications and accountability. (Goldman Sachs, 2015)

Recently, in *Ed in the Apple* (2015), the problems faced by new teachers (and even the experienced ones) were discussed, using a model that may be helpful to new teachers and their supervisors:

> The Dunning-Kruger effect, named after David Dunning and Justin Kruger of Cornell University, occurs where people fail adequately to assess their level of competence—or specifically, their incompetence—at a task and thus consider themselves much more competent than everyone else. This lack of awareness is attributed to their lower level of competence robbing them of the ability critically to analyze their performance, leading to a significant overestimate of themselves. (March 19, 2015)

New teachers do not always know what to try in a classroom. For trying some things (action research), they should have the approval of administration, including perhaps the department chair and the principal. For instance, if the new teacher wants to use one novel with one sophomore class and a different novel with the other sophomore class, the new teacher should probably get approval before complaints from students and parents start coming to the administration.

Or why not videotape a lesson and review the lesson online or on tape and (1) let the teacher critique the lesson, along with the supervisor; (2) work together to make suggestions for improvement; (3) show the teacher other tapes of colleagues handling similar problems and teaching similar lessons; and (4) let new teachers observe experienced ones to get ideas. If the school is a middle or high school, teachers could observe their students taking another class with a different teacher to get hints on how to present, discipline, involve, and improve their techniques.

For instance, a new teacher cannot always "see" what s/he is doing in the classroom and the effects those actions may have on students. Someone in leadership, observing that new teacher in the classroom, can be a new set of eyes to see and point out what is happening. One day I was visiting the classes of my new teachers. As the teacher was teaching in the front of the room, students in the back of the room were doing their homework for another class. The new teacher stayed only in front of the room.

When we spoke together after the class, I mentioned this to the new teacher. She did not see this stationary location that I observed in her classroom. We talked about the importance of "walking around the classroom" while she teaches. This is a real, living example of how those in a leadership position can help new teachers see why students may not be learning—something the new teacher may not notice.

WHAT PRINCIPALS CAN DO TO SUPPORT TEACHERS USING ACTION RESEARCH

Principals and administrators can support new and nearly new teachers by encouraging them to reflect on their practices and determine what is working toward student learning and what obstacles are preventing student learning. This is how teachers (and administrators) use action research. Mills (2014) defines action research in this way:

> Action research is any systematic inquiry conducted by teacher researchers, principals, school counselors, or other stakeholders in the teaching/learning environment to gather information about how their particular schools operate, how they teach, and how well their students learn. This information is gathered with the goals of gaining insight, developing reflective practice, effecting positive changes in the school environment (and on educational practices in general), and improving student outcomes and the lives of those involved. Action research is done *by* teachers *for* themselves; it is not imposed on them by someone else. (p. 8)

Teachers who are supported in an environment that has a vision of academic success for all students, work in a climate hospitable to education, are cultivated as leaders, and are focused on improving instruction using available data are in a prime environment for cultivating student learning and teacher development. Even principals new to administration can introduce this means of reflective practice to all teachers.

Pat Goldys describes how she introduced her teachers to action research as a means to collaborate with other teachers in finding ways to improve instruction and create a community of learners. Within her first year, she worked with teams of teachers who introduced and monitored innovative projects to meet reading and math needs of students. By the end of that year, data revealed that 75 percent of the 620 students benefited from the teachers' action research projects (Goldys, Kruft, & Subrizi, 2007).

Supportive principals and administrative teams who are focused on student learning can support teachers and help them improve practice.

GOING "UP AND UP"

Thus, to improve, our schools, their teachers, administrators, and students must work together to improve everyone's experience and bring them up to speed. This upward process (up is up) could and would involve five upward steps:

- *Matching Up*—Clearly, schools should strive to "match up" good teachers with new and less-experienced, less successful ones, to collaborate and help each other improve. As we have seen, these changes and improvements may be minor, as "moving around the classroom" during lessons and giving students a chance to work together for each other's good, as follows:

  (a) Matching up can start at the top, where outstanding leaders are matched to schools that are struggling and need improvement.
  (b) Matching up teachers with common interests but who may be different in their background, ethnicity, race, and skills.
  (c) Putting them together in teams can improve their performance and make them feel more collegial and, yes, more "professional." Matching up can make a difference in schools' colleagueship, activities, and learning outcomes. Try it.

- *Adding Up*—When schools, students, and their teachers begin to improve, we need to "add up" the results and tell the story. Often good performance and outstanding results are hidden or lost in the busy world, and schools have rarely celebrated their quality jobs and institutional betterment.

We need (a) to invent ways to let everyone know how our schools are doing, (b) to celebrate the improvements, and (c) to become aware of what is working or not. Adding up can give evidence of real growth or of none. Either way, we need to know and see what can be done to do even better.

- *Fixing Up*—The reform steps also obviously include fixing and improving teaching, learning, and thus student/school performance. Once we start up the train of improvement of our schools and student outcomes, it becomes obvious what needs repairs, changes, and improvements. All teachers should write a story of how they have learned to teach—and those moments that tested them and taught them to teach better.

  And importantly, school leaders and coordinators (starting at the top with the principals) should bring together their staff and discuss what's working for each of them and how they can *help each other* to improve. Experienced teachers may be getting tired of instructing the same subjects in the same ways, and newer teachers can learn what works from their elders and inspire senior teachers to try new curricula and pedagogy in classes. Sharing is critical for making teachers better, more professional, and more excited and exciting.

- *Up Is Up*—And finally, good schools are exciting, precious places for staff, students, and societies. The *up is up* will excite and benefit the 3S's, our staff, students, and our societies. No doubt about that. Good leadership works for all, benefiting teachers, students, and the entire school. As the Wallace Foundation found:

  > Today, improving school leadership ranks high on the list of priorities for school reform. In a detailed 2010 survey, school and district administrators, policymakers and others declared principal leadership as among the most pressing matters on a list of issues in public school education. Teacher quality stood above everything else, but principal leadership came next, out-stripping subjects including dropout rates, STEM (science, technology, engineering and math) education, student testing, and preparation for college and careers. (Simkin, Charner, & Suss, 2010, p. 3)

- *Flying Up and Up*—We will end up with a *flying up* as schools, students, and societies improve. No doubt about that. We should welcome everyone into the process if we hope for Upping our Schools: e.g., the students, staff, parents, and citizens. Good schools are always remembered and never forgotten. Up is up!

REFERENCES

Breidenstein, A., Fahey, K., Glickman, C., & Hensley, F. (2012). *Leading for power-ful learning: A guide for instructional leaders.* New York: Teachers College Press.

Carver, C. L. (2003). Chapter 4. The principal's role in new teacher induction. In *Keeping Good Teachers* (Marge Scherer, editor). Washington, DC: Association for Supervision and Curriculum Development.

Collins, J. (2001). *Good to great.* New York: Harper Collins Publishers.

Darling-Hammond, L. (1997). *Doing what matters most: Investing in quality teaching.* Kutztown, PA: National Commission on Teaching and America's Future.

Ed in the Apple. (March 19, 2015). *What is the "New Teacher" crisis? Should we set high barriers to becoming a teacher or figure out how to retain new teachers? Explor-ing the Dunning-Kruger syndrome.* Accessed from https://mets2006.wordpress .com/2015/03/19/what-is-the-new-teacher-crisis-should-we-set-high-barriers -to-becoming-a-teacher-or-figure-out-how-to-retain-new-teachers-exploring -the-dunning-kruger-syndrome/.

Goldman Sachs. (2015). Supporting the Harlem Children's Zone. Retrieved from http://www.goldmansachs.com/citizenship/goldman-sachs-gives/building -and-stabilizing-communities/hcz/.

Goldys, P., Kruft, C., & Subrizi, P. (2007). Action research: Do it yourself. *Principal,* March–April 2007, 60–63.

Ingersoll, R. M. (2001). Teacher turnover and teacher shortages. *American Educa-tional Research Journal, 38*(3), 499–534.

Louis, K. S., Leithwood, K., Anderson, S. E., & Wahlstrom, K. L. (2010). *Learning from leadership: Investigating the links to improved student learning: Final report of research to the Wallace Foundation,* University of Minnesota and University of Toronto, 2010, 9.

Marzano, R. J., Waters, T., & McNulty, B. A. (2005). *School leadership that works: From research to results.* ERIC, Washington, DC: Association for Supervision and Curriculum Development

McEwan, E. K. (2003). *Ten traits of highly effective principals: From good to great per-formance.* Thousand Oaks, CA: Corwin Press.

Mills, G. E. (2014). *Action research: A guide for the teacher researcher.* New York: Pearson.

M. Jacobs, personald communication, April 21, 2008.

National Association of Elementary School Principals. (2008). *Leading learning communities: Standards for what principals should know and be able to do.* Alexan-dria, VA: National Association of Elementary School Principals.

Porter, A., Murphy, J., Goldring, E., Elliott, S. N., Morgan, S., Polikoff, M. S., & May, H. (2008). *Vanderbilt assessment of leadership in education.* Technical manual.

Porter, A. C., Goldring, E. B., Elliott, S. N., Murphy, J., Polikoff, M., and Cravens, X. (2008). *Setting performance standards for the VAL-ED Assessment of Principal Leadership.* New York: Wallace Foundation.

Shute, J., & Cooper, B. S. (2014). *Fixing truancy now: Inviting students back to class.* Lanham, MD: Rowman & Littlefield.

Shute, J., & Cooper, B. S. (2015). Understanding in-school truancy. *Phi Delta Kap-pan, 96,* 65–68.

Simkin, L, Charner, I., & Suss, L. (2010). *Emerging education issues: Findings from The Wallace Foundation Survey*. Prepared for the Wallace Foundation by the Academy for Educational Development, unpublished, 2010, 9–10.

Wallace Foundation. (2013). *The school principal as leader: Guiding schools to better teaching and learning*. New York: Wallace Foundation.

Wallace Foundation (2010). *The three essentials: Improving schools requires district vision, district and state support, and principal leadership*. New York: Wallace Foundation.

Whyte, W. H. (1956). *The organization man*. New York: Simon & Schuster.

II

SIX STEPS IN THE
PROCESS OF *L.E.A.D.E.R.*

In part II of this book, we walk through the six steps of action research, starting with the *L*—meaning *Looking* at the problem—as the first step in *L.E.A.D.E.R.* in chapter 5. We go back to the origin of teaching and pedagogy to show both the importance of this process and the limitations of being a "semiprofession." Chapters 6 through 10 introduce each of the *L.E.A.D.E.R.* steps, including *E* for *examining* what is known; *A* for acquiring new knowledge and methods for handling problems; *D* for *devising* a plan; *E* for *executing and evaluating* the plan; and *R* for repeating the steps as needed.

4

✦

Building a Program for Teachers and Students

Six Steps to Becoming a Classroom L.E.A.D.E.R.

Our twenty-first-century schools need teacher leaders who in turn will cultivate student leaders. Too few students are graduating from college, and too many students who do graduate are underprepared, lacking the proficiencies needed for twenty-first-century work and citizenship (Gaston, 2015).

Among students who begin their education at community colleges with the intent of earning a four-year degree, only one in seven students—and fewer than one in ten Latino or African-American students—have completed the degree after six years (Hillman et al., 2014). For students who do graduate, there is "abundant evidence that too many students are falling short" in terms of learning gains and outcomes (Finley, 2012, p. vii; Bok, 2006; General Education Maps, 2015).

While this recent report from the Association of American Colleges and Universities is disturbing for what recent graduates are prepared to know and do upon completing college, this reality is more concerning for the next generation of teachers. These are the professionals who will teach the next generation.

BUILDING A PROGRAM FOR TEACHER CANDIDATES

Most teacher education programs include some aspect of clinical work within the courses of study. Clinical work may include observation hours in actual classrooms as well as a student teaching experience of one or two semesters. Teacher educators move very quickly from being students (K–16) to teaching students. After a four-year undergraduate program, these candidates assume a full responsibility of teaching students—and hopefully leading them to learning.

It has been said that the best teacher is experience (Gilpin, 2007). Teacher candidates cannot be given experience. And while clinical experiences are certainly beneficial to teacher candidates, they are not considered scholarship until they undergo a systemic reflective analysis. In his work with the Carnegie Foundation for the Advancement of Teaching, Lee Shulman (2000) advocates that this reflection leads to a "display or communication in ways that render it community property in the fullest sense—public, reviewed and exchanged" (p. 50).

At the undergraduate level, clinical experiences can provide some of these opportunities. Kuh (2008) lists learning communities, writing-intensive courses, collaborative assignments and projects, undergraduate research, and service learning among the practices that contribute to students' cumulative learning.

Goals for learning communities include integrating learning across two or more courses and involving students with major questions beyond the classroom. In courses that include intensive writing, students produce and revise various forms of writing for various audiences across disciplines.

Students collaborate to work and solve problems as they gain insights from others, especially those with different backgrounds and life experiences. Research involves students with "actively contested questions, empirical observation, cutting-edge technologies, and the sense of excitement that comes from working to answer important questions" in direct experiences they are studying by analyzing and solving problems within the community. Students apply what they are learning to real-life situations (Kuh, 2008, p. 1).

New and nearly new teachers need these experiences—and preferably before they reach their own classrooms. Teachers who graduate with an inquiry sense—a sense of excitement in determining and answering important questions—are already on a pathway to become a teacher *L.E.A.D.E.R.*

Thus, this chapter focuses on the real process and steps in action research that can guide teachers, administrators, and even parents—and students—in solving their own problems and improving their learning and assessing. Teaching staff, teachers, students, and family will come to understand the research process, around these six steps: (1) $L = Look$ at the problem; (2) $E = Examine$ what we know; (3) $A = Acquire$ knowledge of school problem solving; (4) $D = Devise$ a plan for improvement; (5) $E = Execute$ the plan; and, (6) $R = Repeat$ steps and processes as needed.

WHERE DO WE FIND PROBLEM SOLVERS?

Problem solvers are not a special breed in the population. We are born problem solvers. Ask a mother of a two-year-old and she will tell us that her child can solve any problem: getting out of a crib, reaching objects that are not within reach, sampling any kind of solids or liquids that may resemble something to eat or drink. Two-year-olds find a way to solve any problem that is of interest. So what happens? When do children lose the drive, curiosity, and the ability to problem solve?

As a principal of a PK-Grade 8 school in central New Jersey, the teachers and I asked ourselves this question. Why do our students look to us to solve their problems? Why aren't they solving their own problems? At first this was an informal conversation; but as the same conversation surfaced time and time again, our question became more serious. Students seemed to not be able to take steps to solve a problem on their own and were even more content to let an adult solve the problem for them.

When we began the process of a school self-study, we asked ourselves the question: What is a major issue we are facing that is preventing our students from learning and becoming competent young people? The answer: problem solving! The staff noted multiple instances of students not taking initiative in solving their own issues:

- Can I call my mother? She forgot to pack my gym clothes.
- Nobody will play with me (playground).
- There's nothing to do out here (also playground with slides, swings, sandbox, jungle gym, Nerf balls . . .).
- This (math) problem is too hard.
- I don't have a pencil.

These were typical comments heard on a daily basis. As a staff we recognized that if our students could not find ways to solve their problems at this level, they would struggle to meet social and academic challenges in the future.

As a faculty we decided to design our accreditation project with a program to promote student problem solvers and leaders. This became an endeavor which encompassed families as well as all students and staff. The project became known as *L.E.A.D.E.R.*

WHY WE NEED PROBLEM SOLVERS

According to the U.S. Department of Labor, the average worker will hold more than ten jobs before the age of forty. The top ten "in-demand" jobs projected for 2010 did not exist in 2004. For twenty-first-century students, learning cannot be the same as it was for those who teach these students. A growing body of research has shown the following:

> Students learn more deeply when they can apply classroom-gathered knowledge to real-world problems, and when they take part in projects that require sustained engagement and collaboration. Active-learning practices have a more significant impact on student performance than any other variable, including student background and prior achievement. Students are most successful when they are taught how to learn as well as what to learn. (Darling-Hammond et al., 2008, introduction, para. 3–4)

Furthermore, researchers found:

> We are doing a poor job of moving capable students into the highest levels of achievement. For capable, culturally different, and low-income students, the results are deplorable. For example, national and state data on the National Assessment of Education Progress (NAEP) exams reveal that not only are we moving only small numbers of students to the advanced level but we are also moving far fewer culturally different and low-income students to those levels. The difference is an example of an achievement gap dubbed, the "excellence gap." (Olszewski-Kubilius & Clarenbach, 2014, p. 104).

Recognizing that our young people today need skills beyond what we are even imagining in classrooms presently led the faculty to the awareness that these students had to be thinking beyond the here and now. They had to have the abilities to solve nonconventional problems that had not yet been imagined. Students had to pose questions and use inquiry to lead to new solutions. This would not happen automatically—especially if they were in a mindset to let adults solve problems for them.

Not only was it necessary to introduce the skills associated with problem solving—e.g., collaboration, innovation, logic, flexibility, deep and creative thinking, alternative approaches—but also the reality that a solution to a problem could not be taught in a classroom setting.

With the research in mind, the faculty designed a six-step process based on scientific inquiry that the school community—students, teachers, staff, and families—would follow to solve their own problems and problems they shared in common. The acronym *L.E.A.D.E.R.* gave the steps in the problem-solving practice:

L—Look at the problem
E—Examine what I know
A—Acquire knowledge
D—Devise a plan
E—Execute the plan
R—Repeat the steps as needed and PERSEVERE!

INTRODUCING *L.E.A.D.E.R.*

Students had to be taught how to apply the six steps of *L.E.A.D.E.R.* in many different situations. Faculty and staff devised problem-solving tasks but more often used problem-solving opportunities that presented themselves on a daily basis to teach and utilize the necessary steps. Each morning during assembly, the school community recited together: *I am a problem solver and leader. I look at the problem, examine what I know, acquire knowledge, devise a plan, execute the plan, and repeat the steps as needed and persevere.* Within weeks, the entire school community could recite the six steps to problem solving. That was the easy part. The hard work began with implementing the process.

As a staff, we decided we would start with a schoolwide project—garbage. Our problem question was "What do we do with all this garbage?" To introduce the students to the concept of problem solving, we had a school assembly where each class was challenged with the same math problem:

> Farmer Joe has a problem. He has chickens and pigs in his barnyard and he needs to count them. He knows there are 60 legs and 22 heads. Can you help Farmer Joe count his chickens and pigs?

Students were told they could use anything in their classroom (except the Internet) to solve the problem. They had to show all their work, and when they had the problem solved, they had to come back to the gym and be ready to explain how they helped Farmer Joe.

Grade 6 was the first class to return with their solution—followed by grade 1. Once all classes were assembled again, representatives from grades 6 and 1 went onto the stage to explain their solution. As expected, grade 6 used a mathematical approach involving basic algebraic equations. They did not know how to use a system of equations for solving the problem but were able to use guess and check to find a solution.

Grade 1 had a different approach. They used their snap cubes to create two-legged and four-legged models and kept combining them until they had sixty legs with twenty-two heads. Both classes had the correct number for Farmer Joe. Both classes explained how they solved their problem. As the students explained their processes, we wrote their steps on the computer and projected it on the screen. Of course their steps were *L.E.A.D.E.R.* And so *L.E.A.D.E.R.* was born.

Students' next project was to create a poster that would illustrate these steps and that they could display in their classrooms and throughout the school. Melissa, the art teacher, took their design plans and created our official poster.

IMPLEMENTING *L.E.A.D.E.R.*

Within a week of the assembly we reconvened the whole school to introduce our schoolwide project on garbage: What do we do with all this garbage? Each class was challenged to solve the problem of garbage using the steps in the *L.E.A.D.E.R.* format. Teachers assisted their classes in addressing various aspects of garbage as it related to the school.

Classes explored many options, including schoolwide recycling that involved getting the city to provide recycling containers for classrooms, general gathering spaces such as the lunchroom, and outdoors to hold the recyclables until the designated collection day. The cafeteria changed from Styrofoam and plastics to silverware and serving trays that were sent daily through the dishwasher. Preschoolers dabbled in paper making that they gave as Mother's Day gifts; first-graders tabulated the total number of snack containers they generated in a week; and fifth-graders carried around their own garbage, which resulted in generating composting in a school garden.

While the focus was on the garbage project, teachers incorporated the six steps in the more common problems students encountered every day. The first approach to problem solving involved social issues: classroom conflicts—line cutting, taking turns, listening—and individual challenges—completing homework, having required supplies, being on time. Gradually teachers involved students with using the six steps in academic issues such as recognizing and applying the steps in math, science, and social studies. Teachers adapted the *L.E.A.D.E.R.* steps as a format for word problems, as an inquiry approach in science, and as an investigation for resolving world conflicts.

Eventually parents and guardians were brought on board in using *L.E.A.D.E.R.* At a home/school meeting, attendees were given the same problem to help Farmer Joe and to work with other parents in solving the problem. Students taught the audience the six steps of *L.E.A.D.E.R.*, gave each family a miniature-size copy of the poster to be posted in a prominent place in the home, and encouraged families to use the model to solve home problems and challenges.

L.E.A.D.E.R ON A DAILY BASIS

While developing the garbage project focused the entire school community on one big problem, using *L.E.A.D.E.R.* on a daily basis required awareness and retraining on the part of the teachers. Teachers had to stop solving students' problems for them.

The faculty discussed ways to implement *L.E.A.D.E.R.* on a daily basis. They developed a "problem-solving language" that included asking appropriate questions such as: What is the problem? Is this really a problem? How is this problem? Why is this problem? The most important component of *L.E.A.D.E.R.* was identifying the problem. Teachers found that any issues that students found to be not to their liking they considered a problem. Distinguishing between real problems and inconveniences helped students and teachers more clearly identify problems.

By the end of the first school year using *L.E.A.D.E.R.*, students, teachers, parents, and staff were more frequently using these six steps to help them consciously and systematically solve problems personally, in classrooms, at home, and within the community. Each year thereafter, the school community focused on another problem that related directly to the school community. Projects included designing a safer recreation area for students on school grounds, an awareness campaign for combating bullying in and outside of school, and soil testing for greener gardens. Each problem and project resulted in a public display of learning, review, and exchanging of ideas.

TEACHERS AS *L.E.A.D.E.R.*S

The story above retells how one school implemented *L.E.A.D.E.R.* into its program at the schoolwide level as well as the classroom level. Students as well as teachers, staff, and parents worked together to change a school culture from dependent to independent problem solvers and leaders. Each step in the *L.E.A.D.E.R.* process promotes a skill set that enhances leadership capabilities.

Before teachers can teach *L.E.A.D.E.R.*, teachers need to inculcate the principles of this format into their own practices. This may be particularly challenging for new and nearly new teachers. School leaders are often regarded as the principal or those in administration—department chairs, assistant principals—those who supervise other staff within the school. But true leadership comes from within and is often cultivated by outstanding teacher leaders.

The classroom teacher is a leader. Katie Haycock is referenced in the 2008 Wallace Foundation describing leaders in this way:

> When you meet the leaders in the places that are really getting the job done, they are not the kind of leaders that just turn things around by the sheer force of their personality. They are regular people. They are totally focused. They are totally relentless. They are not big, outsized personalities and they are not the only leaders in their schools. Especially in the larger schools,

the principals know that they can't get it all done themselves. Those are the places that improve. Leadership is not about one person; it's about building a shared commitment and building a leadership team. (p. 2)

In her study on school leadership Clayton (2014) found that the skills, knowledge, and attitudes critical to leaders in schools today include instructional leadership, ethical decision making, cultural competency, and organizational management. These elements are just as important in the classroom as they are in the school at large. In fact, if these elements are not present among leaders in classrooms, the probability of leadership throughout the school is diminished.

HOW TEACHERS DEVELOP AS LEADERS

Teacher leaders take ownership of their classes and assume responsibility for student learning as well as their own learning. They do not provide excuses to explain why students "can't"—but rather look for how students "can." Elaine McEwan (2002) in her book *Ten Traits of Highly Effective Teachers* lists the following traits:

- Mission Driven and Passionate—The effective teacher is mission driven, feeling a call to teach as well as a passion to help students learn and grow.
- Positive and Real—The highly effective teacher is positive and real, demonstrating the qualities of caring, empathy, respect, and fairness in relationships with students, parents, and colleagues.
- A Teacher Leader—The highly effective teacher is a teacher leader who positively affects the lives of students, parents, and colleagues.
- With-It-Ness—The highly effective teacher demonstrates with-it-ness: the state of being on top of it, tuned in to, aware of, and in complete control of three critical facets of classroom life: • The management and organization of the classroom • The engagement of students • The management of time.
- Style—The effective teacher exhibits his or her own unique style, bringing drama, enthusiasm, liveliness, humor, charisma, creativity, and novelty to his or her teaching.
- Motivational Expertise—The highly effective teacher is a motivator par excellence who believes in his or her own ability to make a difference in the lives of students and relentlessly presses and pursues students to maintain the highest possible behavioral and academic standards.
- Instructional Effectiveness—The highly effective teacher is an instructional virtuoso: a skilled communicator with a repertoire of essential abilities, behaviors, models, and principles that lead all students to learning.

- Book Learning—The highly effective teacher has a sound knowledge of content (the structure of the discipline) and outcomes (what the school, district, or state has determined is essential for students to know).
- Street Smarts—The highly effective teacher has knowledge of the students, the school, and the community in which he or she is teaching and uses this knowledge to solve problems in the instructional setting.
- A Mental Life—The highly effective teacher has a substantive thought life that includes the abilities to be the following: • *Metacognitive*: able to read one's own mental state and then assess how the state will affect one's present and future performance • *Strategic*: able to think aloud and model strategic learning for students • *Reflective*: able to think about personal teaching behaviors for the purposes of self-growth • *Communicative*: able to articulate ideas, issues, beliefs, and values about the act of teaching with colleagues, students, and parents • *Responsive*: able to flex to the changing needs and demands of the profession.

(McEwan, 191–193)

Dixon's (2012) study of principals' perspectives on the quality of effective teachers supports McEwan's descriptions. She found that based on her study and the review of research, effective teachers exhibit these qualities:

> knowledgeable of subject matter, excellent communication skills, positive rapport with students, compassionate and understanding, passionate about teaching, resourceful and creative, a life-long learner, inspiring and motivational, results-oriented, teacher-leader, open-minded and flexible, effective classroom management, and high expectations for learning. (p. 27)

Effective teachers are teacher leaders—in their classrooms, in their schools, and in their communities. They lead themselves, they lead others, and they lead with others. They are at the forefront as problem solvers because they assume responsibility for what is happening. They do not wait to be told to go ahead; they lead the pack.

Teacher leaders find schools that support their teaching mission. They are not satisfied with taking the first offer of a job, although they may take that offer. Once they have acquired a position, they constantly determine a match between their personal mission and the mission of the school. When those missions are aligned, they make learning happen. When the missions are mismatched, they take steps to align personal mission with the school mission without compromising their values and ethics. If this is not possible, they have the courage to move on and find the place where they can lead learning with other colleagues who share a common mission.

FOLLOWING THE STEPS OF *L.E.A.D.E.R.*

The steps of the *L.E.A.D.E.R.* program support teachers and students in resolving their own problems through a process that equates with action research. From the first step in the process of defining the problem, teachers assume an inquiry stance to determine the issue that needs to be resolved. Students follow in the same format as they identify the real problem they are facing. As teachers gather information that will help them understand the problem, students in turn do the same.

Once teachers have a clear idea of the problem and understand what they already know about the problem, they consult with other experts in the field to study what others have done to solve similar problems. Students consult with others who may assist them in acquiring new knowledge about the problem and determining ways to handle the problem. With this new knowledge, a plan is proposed for addressing the problem and steps are taken to put the plan in action.

Throughout the plan, teacher leaders gather data that help them decide the effectiveness of the plan and assists them to decide next steps. They use those data to determine what steps in the plan need to be repeated and what steps to take next in moving forward in solving the problem. This reflective process "has the potential to lead to significant growth as these thoughtful considerations of . . . teaching and student learning will lay the groundwork for a successful career in education" (Henniger, 2004, p. 369).

Sometimes problems can be solved in a simple commonsense approach, but sometimes a more systematic approach is needed. The six steps in *L.E.A.D.E.R.* provide that systematic approach which leads to using action research in solving a problem at a local level and in a very specific situation, or at a schoolwide level. The intent is not to generalize findings to a broad audience, but to address a local issue and share those findings with interested individuals.

Kemmis (2010) concludes that educational action research demands a series of commitments. Action research is a journey through self-reflective inquiry that is shared publicly. Action research is conducted to improve teaching and self. Action research is undertaken to improve practice—the practice of teaching and learning for teachers, for students, and for the learning community.

The next six chapters in this book give the detailed steps in the *L.E.A.D.E.R.* process and provide practical applications of each step.

Several online surveys are available to assess problem-solving capabilities:

1. Queendom's Creative Problem-Solving Test—http://www.queendom .com/tests/access_page/index.htm?idRegTest=2286#n
2. Human Service Research Problem-Solving Survey—used with 4H— http://www.humanserviceresearch.com/youthlifeskillsevaluation/ problem.pdf
3. Problem Solving and Logical Reasoning Survey for middle school students—http://www.strivetogether.org/sites/default/files/im ages/11%20PSLR_Problem%20Solving%20and%20Logical%20Reason ing%20Survey.pdf (Poynton, Carlson, Hopper, & Carey, 2006)
4. School districts created their own surveys to assess their problem-solving approaches—http://www.rtinetwork.org/images/content/downloads/ get%20started/sapsi_form.pdf (RTI Action Network, 2015)

REFERENCES

Bok, D. (2006). *Our underachieving colleges: A candid look at how much students learn and why they should be learning more.* Princeton, NJ: Princeton University Press.

Clayton, J. K. (2014). The leadership lens: Perspectives on leadership from school district personnel and university faculty. *International Journal of Educational Leadership Preparation, 9*(1), 17. Retrieved from http://search.proquest.com/do cview/1651832159?accountid=12258.

Darling-Hammond, L., Barron, B., Pearson, P. D., Schoenfeld, A. H., Stage, E. K., Zimmerman, T. D., Cervetti, G. N., & Tilson, J. L. (2008). *Powerful learning: What we know about teaching for understanding.* San Francisco: Jossey-Bass.

Dixon, A. J. (2012). *School principal perspectives on the qualities of highly effective teachers: Are there distinguishing characteristics?* Retrieved from http://www.nwmis souri.edu/library/fieldstudies/2012/Dixon,%20Andrea%20J.pdf.

Finley, A. (2012). *Making progress? What we know about the achievement of liberal education outcomes.* Washington, DC: Association of American Colleges and Universities.

Gaston, P. (2015). *General education transformed: How we can, why we must.* Washington, DC: Association of American Colleges and Universities.

General education maps and markers: Designing meaningful pathways to student achievement. (2015). Washington, DC: Association of American Colleges and Universities. Retrieved from https://www.aacu.org/sites/default/files/files/ publications/GenEdDesignPrinciples.pdf.

Gilpin, L. S. (2007). Unearthing the scholarship of teaching and learning in self and practice. *International Journal for the Scholarship of Teaching and Learning, 2*(1), 125–35.

Henniger, M. L. (2004). *The teaching experience: An introduction to reflective practice.* Upper Saddle River, NJ: Pearson.

Hillman, M., Quigley, P., Safman, P., Shea, P., & Turner, R. (2014). *Successful student transfer: A key building block for the completion agenda.* Retrieved from http://www.wiche.edu/content/successful-student-transfer-key-building -block-completion-agenda.

Kemmis, S. (2010). Research for praxis: Knowing doing. *Pedagogy, Culture & Society, 18*(1), 9–27.

Kuh, G. D. (2008). *High impact educational practices: What they are, who has access to them, and why they matter.* Washington, DC: Association of American Colleges and Universities.

McEwan, E. (2002). *Ten traits of highly effective teachers: How to hire, coach, and mentor successful teachers.* Thousand Oaks, CA: Corwin.

Olszewski-Kubilius, P., & Clarenbach, J. (2014). Closing the opportunity gap: Program factors contributing to academic success in culturally different youth. *Gifted Child Today, 37*(2), 102–10. Retrieved from http://search.proquest.com/ docview/1532147727?accountid=12258.

Poynton, T. A., Carlson, M. W., Hopper, J. A., & Carey, J. C. (2006). Evaluation of an innovative approach to improving middle school students' academic achievement. *Professional School Counseling*, 10962409. Retrieved from http://www .strivetogether.org/sites/default/files/images/11%20PSLR_Problem%20Solv ing%20and%20Logical%20Reasoning%20Survey.pdf.

RTI Action Network. (2015). *Self-assessment of problem solving implementation (SAPSI).* New York: National Center for Learning Disabilities. Retrieved from http://www.rtinetwork.org/images/content/downloads/get%20started/ sapsi_form.pdf.

Shulman, L. (2000). From Minsk to Pinsk: Why scholarship of teaching and learning? *Journal of Scholarship of Teaching and Learning, 1*(1), 48–53.

Wallace Foundation. (2008). *Becoming a leader: Preparing school principals for today's schools.* Retrieved from http://www.wallacefoundation.org/knowledge -center/school-leadership/principal-training/Documents/Becoming-a -Leader-Preparing-Principals-for-Todays-Schools.pdf.

5

Looking at the Problem

Teachers face challenges in the classroom every day. Some are spur-of-the-moment challenges (e.g., Sandy and Alan are disagreeing over whose turn it is to collect papers). Some are long-term challenges (e.g., KC, Kevin, and Julie did not complete homework again). Some have an easy fix, while a number require more strategic planning and doing. The first step in meeting the challenge is determining the problem.

A SAMPLE PROBLEM

Pat's English class has twenty-eight freshmen, perfectly segmented into fourteen male and fourteen female students. He is almost through the first month of school, and he is still trying to figure out what makes this group tick—or not. He strongly supports a Socratic seminar–type class setting in which students collaboratively dialogue through facilitated open-ended questions about text (Roberts & Billings, 2012). This approach integrates reading, writing, listening, and speaking. Students are required to read and annotate texts prior to the class and come to class prepared to discuss the text.

Students write a short reflective piece before class, responding to the question posed by the teacher. Students reference the text in their reflective piece, indicating the word, sentence, or paragraph that supports their reflective response. During seminar, students sit in a circle so they can see and interact with each other. They are allowed to have their reflective piece with them during the seminar, which begins with a recap of the text by one assigned student, and then Pat poses the question students used in their reflective piece.

Pat is puzzled by what follows—silence. That silence can continue anywhere from thirty seconds to four minutes (and may even be longer if Pat does not break the silence with another question or suggested prompt). What's the problem here? Pat has been asking himself that question for at least three weeks. He also has been trying to answer his question: perhaps the reading is too hard; perhaps this group is very shy; perhaps this is a low-performing group; or perhaps this group expects the teacher to do more talking. But he has yet to determine what the real problem is.

When teachers meet such challenges in their classrooms, often they seek solutions before they have clearly identified the problem. Pat is often fixing the problem before he even knows what the problem is. How can you fix the problem without first knowing the problem?

A MODEL FOR CLASSROOM PERFORMANCE

Unfortunately, Pat's approach is not uncommon among teachers—especially new teachers. Performances in the classroom are multifaceted. More than thirty years ago Hoy and Forsyth (1986) described what they called the systems model of classroom performance. The model includes five performance components of classrooms that they proposed need to be in congruence for effective teaching and learning to take place. The five components are: teacher, student, task, formal organization, and climate.

When considering the teacher, the emphasis is on the personal characteristics of the teacher—i.e., the teacher's knowledge, skills, and values as well as the teacher's perceptions and expectations. Personal characteristics of students are also central to effective classroom performance. Students bring their knowledge, skills, values, and abilities to the classroom. Students have perceptions and expectations of their school, teachers, peers, and themselves that influence performance.

Teaching in the classroom can be categorized into skill learning, knowledge learning, and value learning. Thus, the strategy chosen to promote learning depends on the type of learning expected. Teachers are trying to promote learning and thus select strategies to meet that goal.

The fourth component is the formal organization of the classroom—i.e., structures, processes, and materials. These include the structure of the activities (classroom rules and procedures); the instructional methods (discussion, lecture, inquiry, drill); and the materials, such as books, used in teaching.

The fifth component is the class climate—the informal socialization that goes on among students and teacher. While the teacher is expected to formally lead the class, informal student leaders are also present. As students interact in the formal school setting, informal norms and leadership patterns emerge that affect behavior in the classroom (Hoy & Forsyth, 1986).

To determine the problem in the classroom, the teacher researcher needs to examine the congruency among the five components of the systems model of classroom performance. Each component needs to be aligned with each other component. If there is a discrepancy among any of the components, there is likely to be a problem. The question for each component is, what is expected? The reality is what is happening.

The teacher has expectations in each component. Pat has certain expectations about this class. Pat expects his students to have the skills and knowledge to read the assigned text and analyze the text in reflective writing. He expects the students to value the learning that is a part of this experience and therefore to come prepared for class. He values the Socratic style of this task that requires reading and writing and then listening and speaking as part of the seminar.

Pat organizes the class in a circle, hoping it is best for this task, as it allows all students to see each other. He trusts that students respect each other and that they will demonstrate this respect as they contribute their own ideas and listen to the ideas of their classmates in the seminar. In this case it seems that Pat's expectations are a reality of what is happening. Figure 5.1 shows the alignment between what Pat expects and the reality in the classroom.

Pat (teacher)	Expectation	Reality
Students	Come prepared—read text; contribute to discussion	√
Task	Completed reflection	√
Organization	Sit in circle to enable all to see each other	√
Climate	Respectful	√

Figure 5.1. Expectation and Reality Alignment between Teacher and Components

FOCUSING ON THE PROBLEM

But Pat is only part of the whole picture, as four other components have to be in alignment also. Since students have expectations, the format of the task is expected to accomplish results; the organization in the classroom needs to support all the elements; and the classroom climate has to be such to support teacher, student, the task, and the formal organization of the classroom.

Each component of this model interacts with every other component. For instance, students' needs must be matched by the task that is under development. In Pat's classroom, he has to find a match between the students' needs and Socratic seminar. While Socratic seminars are researched-based strategies for developing the literacy skills of students, the question here is, can an appropriate match be found between these students and Socratic seminars?

At least two levels of learning with Socratic seminars exist: knowledge learning and skills learning. Pat must ask if these students have the knowledge and the skills to learn effectively from Socratic seminar. If these students do not have the knowledge or the skills, a mismatch between students and task will occur. This *could* be the real problem in Pat's classroom.

This same process of checking for mismatches must be followed for each relationship among the five components. Are the needs of the students in alignment with the needs of the teacher?

While Pat may have the personality that thrives with Socratic seminar, do these students have that kind of personality? Sitting in a circle (the formal organization for this task) has been found effective with other groups who have used Socratic seminars (Roberts & Billings, 2012), but does the circle format match the learning needs and personalities of these students? In the task itself, are the selected texts the students are required to read and discuss aligned with the needs, backgrounds, and interests of these students?

While this process of determining matches and mismatches may seem time-consuming—especially for a new teacher—this is a critical step in identifying the real problem. Hoy and Forsyth (1986) suggest several questions to ask about the connect or disconnect among the components of the model in figure 5.2.

DESCRIBING THE TASK, FORMAL STRUCTURE, AND CLASS CLIMATE

Before beginning to answer the guide questions, the teacher researcher needs to describe in as much detail as possible the task, the formal structure in the classroom, and the class climate. While Pat was very clear in his own mind on the task involving a Socratic seminar, describing the task to a colleague helped him identify specifics of the task, such as text references and the timing of the task. This is how he described what he thought the task was:

Match	Crucial Issues
Teacher ◄──► Climate	To what extent are teacher needs supported by the classroom climate?
Student ◄──► Climate	To what extent are student needs met by the classroom climate?
Teacher ◄──► Task	To what extent are teacher needs met by the teaching task? Does the teacher have the skills and abilities to achieve the task?
Student ◄──► Task	To what extent are student needs met by what is taught? Do students have the abilities and interests to accomplish the task?
Student ◄──► Teacher	To what extent are student and teacher needs consistent?
Task ◄──► Climate	Does the classroom climate facilitate the teaching task? Does the classroom climate hinder or promote the demands of learning?
Task ◄──► Formula Structure	Do the formal classroom arrangements facilitate the teaching-learning process? Do the formal classroom arrangements motivate behavior consistent with the task demands?
Teacher ◄──► Formula Structure	To what extent are teacher needs met by the formal classroom?
Student ◄──► Formula Structure	To what extent are student needs met by the formal classroom arrangements? To what extent do students have a clear perception of classroom expectations— the convergence of student and teacher goals?
Formula Structure ◄──► Climate	To what extent are the goals, rewards, and norms of the informal classroom organization consistent with those of the formal organization?
Classroom ◄──► School	To what extent is the internal structure of the classroom components consistent with the broader school constraints?

Figure 5.2.   Questions Promoting Alignment among System Components
(Hoy & Forsyth, 1986, p. 44)

We are using Socratic seminar to discuss the novel *To Kill a Mockingbird*. We have the seminars on Mondays, and on Fridays I assign the question we will discuss. The question this week was "Did Tom Robinson get a fair trial?" Students answer the question themselves in a written essay of no more than one page. In their essays students define any abstract or ambiguous terms, make direct textual references including the page number, and support their answer with specific evidence from the novel. They are encouraged to reference any discussions from class as part of their response.

Pat goes on to describe the formal organization of the class and the class climate.

I would describe my class as a quiet and reserved group of ninth-graders. As this is their first year in high school and students come from three different middle schools, many of these students did not know each other at the start of the school year. I spent a few days in the first week of school trying to create a class community by including games and strategies that allowed students to get to know each other by name and interests.

We have definite classroom procedures such as assigned seating in quads, but I use group strategies such as partner elbows, think-pair-share, think-pair-square, and jigsaw, which have students move around the classroom and work with other students beyond their quad. We have mutually agreed on having one person speak at a time and use active listening. Students are respectful of each other and of me and demonstrate this by addressing one another by name, looking at the person who is speaking, and helping each other and accepting help from one another.

When task, formal structure, and class climate are described, the next step is to use the guide questions to determine the critical issues. Rewording the guide questions to include personal pronouns (he or she) instead of "teacher" or "student" makes the questions more personal. For example, in the teacher/climate question, rewording the question in this way makes the question more direct: "*To what extent are my needs supported in the classroom climate?*"

The teacher researcher makes note of what the teacher is expecting and what is the reality with the task from these students, and what the expectations and reality are for the students. The teacher then determines what is a match and what is a mismatch. Brief notes in figure 5.3 record Pat's alignment of what he expects and what he is indicating as the reality in this situation. In figure 5.3 he indicates if the expectations are matched or mismatched.

Teacher	Expectation	Reality	Match	Mismatch
1. Teacher	Knowledge, skills, and values	I have knowledge and skills and value Socratic seminar	X	
2. Students	Knowledge, skills, and values	Students do written reflection	X	
3. Task	Participate in Socratic seminar	Students do reflection but do not discuss		X
4. Formal organization	Sit in circle to enable all to see each other	Circle seems okay; students seem comfortable	X	
5. Climate	Respectful and participative	Students have respectful behaviors, but hesitate to speak		X
6. Teacher	To teach and lead the class	Teaches and gives assignments	X	
7. Students	To be respectful of each other	Respectful	X	
8. Task	To respond to given question	Reflection piece is written but not discussed		X
9. Formal organization	Procedures and class rules	Procedures and class rules followed	X	
10. Climate	Work collaboratively	Not working in groups		X

Figure 5.3. Expectation and Reality Alignment

GETTING TO THE PROBLEM

Pat now looks at the alignment of the expectation and reality from his perspective and notices areas that indicate some mismatch between expectation and reality. In Pat's situation the task and climate from his perspective and from what he assumes is the perspective of his students are mismatched. (That is not always the case—what may be a mismatch for the teacher may be a match for the student. That would then be a mismatch between the teacher's and the students' expectations and realities.) From Pat's notes, a few ideas surface: e.g., students do the written reflection, demonstrate respectful behaviors, but do not speak and are not working in groups.

Although the idea of the Socratic seminar is to build understanding of the text together using rigorous and thought-provoking dialogue, the indication of mismatch in task and climate may suggest that these students have insightful ideas based on their own text reading and reflection but are not comfortable with sharing those ideas as a group. The written part of the task is not the problem, because students are completing the assignment. Sharing the written reflection in a whole-group seminar may be the problem.

In looking back at Pat's description of the organization and climate of his class, one notices how he describes the types of group work he uses as a regular part of his classes. He must find that the group work is effective because of how he describes the various formats.

But as Pat thinks about his Socratic seminars, he realizes these are not small-group activities, but rather the whole class working together. Could that be the problem for these students—whole group versus small groups? He describes his students as quiet and reserved, and these characteristics may benefit learning in smaller groups. But these characteristics may not be best in a large group.

Pat is now ready to focus his study.

CREATING A FOCUSED RESEARCH QUESTION

In action research, as in all research, a clear, focused research question is essential. In action research Mills (2014) suggests that the teacher researcher writes an area of focus statement that begins with "the purpose of this study is to . . ." (p. 70). In Pat's case the area of focus statement reads: *The purpose of this study is to determine how using small-group discussion strategies can eventually lead to whole class sharing in Socratic seminar.*

Once the purpose statement (which is the first step to defining the problem) is created, the next step is to generate research questions that will guide the action research. The teacher researcher must realize that the answers to these questions will not be found in other research sources, but rather in the critical thinking the researcher brings to the research.

CREATING RESEARCH QUESTIONS

In thinking about the problem, the researcher determines what it is the researcher wants to know. Various types of questions can emerge, and the teacher will want to be clear on what information is sought. These questions and prompts can help the researcher in formulating the research questions:

1. What is the problem? Explain it to someone who might not have seen or experienced the problem.

2. For whom is the problem a problem?
3. How do these people experience the problem?
4. How are they inconvenienced or harmed by the problem?
5. Who has the power to solve the problem?
6. Why hasn't the problem been solved up to this point?

(Bean, 2011, p. 258)

After responding to these questions, the teacher researcher can formulate his or her own research questions based on the problem.

This is how Pat responded to these questions in a narrative response:

The problem is that students are not participating orally in Socratic seminar. As we read the novel, I assign an open-ended question to the students on Friday, and they have to write their response, including textual references with specific page numbers to support their response. They bring this response to class on Monday and can refer to the response while we sit in a circle so we can easily see each other. Although the students write their response and bring it with them for seminar, there is little to no discussion on the part of the students.

Two groups emerge for whom this problem is a problem: the students and me as the facilitator of the seminar. The students experience this problem when they have long periods of silence (anywhere from thirty seconds up to four minutes on one of the days). These silences seem extreme and a waste of valuable class time. I am as uncomfortable as the students, as I want them to start sharing their ideas so we can begin a discussion. I have read their responses each week, and they have good ideas to share—they just do not share them.

In several ways, the students are being harmed by this problem. They are missing opportunities to develop critical communication skills such as asking thoughtful questions, responding to other points of view, asking clarifying questions, expanding on each other's ideas, and developing leadership. I feel I rescue them by asking lower-level questions they can answer just so someone will start talking. I am feeling frustrated with trying to get this group to participate in a large-group discussion.

I feel I should have the power to solve this problem. I just have to find a way to get these students discussing with each other in a whole-group setting. I have not been able to do that yet because I keep trying to conduct this seminar in this format. Perhaps I need to consider another way to get to the whole class sharing the way I want by looking at what are alternatives to Socratic seminar or by taking smaller steps in the process to get to whole-group sharing.

Pat realizes that his problem is that students are not as comfortable sharing in a large group as they are in a small group. He wants to move them to that comfort level, so he has to find ways to make that happen. His main question is, *How do I get students to discuss in a large-group set-*

ting? His support questions include: What small-group strategies work with these students? How do these strategies work for these students? How can these strategies be adapted to work in a large-group setting?

LOOKING AT THE PROBLEM

When Pat started this process, he identified the problem that he was facing as students were not participating in seminar discussions. As he went through the process of aligning the needs of the students, his own needs, the task, the formal structure, and his classroom climate, his focus changed from the students not doing what he wanted to a new focus on what steps he would take to bring students to a new level of class participation. His problem is one he can solve by changing himself and not expecting others to change.

As Pat now looks at this problem, he can state his problem in a question format that will guide him in finding a solution to the problem. With his problem focused, he now can move on to the next step in examining what he already knows about this problem: How can I get students to discuss in a large group? His three guiding questions—

1. What small-group strategies work with these students?
2. How do these strategies work for these students?
3. How can these strategies be adapted to work in a large-group setting?

—will give him a direction for moving forward in solving his problem.

CHECKING WITH PEERS

In each step on the way to solving various problems, teacher researchers are encouraged to rely on colleagues to review their own thinking by sharing (1) where they are in the process, (2) what they have learned up to this point, and (3) what direction will move them forward. These are some ideas on how to use peer review.

a. Share the narrative question response with the peer review group to describe the teacher researcher's problem. Putting the problem in words for those who are not familiar with the problem forces the teacher researcher to become more focused on the actual problem rather than an assumed problem.

b. Do not tell peers what the main question is. Ask them to phrase key questions about this problem based on the shared narrative response. Determine if peers' questions are similar to the teacher researcher's questions, very different, or if they believe that this is even a problem.

c. While peers like to "fix the problem" by suggesting solutions, avoid reviews moving in that direction. Thank peers for their questions— but do not answer their questions. The teacher researcher examines their questions in light of what the teacher researcher determined to be the problem. This is a good time to revise the main question if questions from peers suggest that. Peers' questions may become additional supporting questions that guide the teacher researcher in the research process.

Before advancing to the next step, be sure that the problem is clearly articulated and is stated in the form of a question.

REFERENCES

Bean, J. C. (2011). *Engaging ideas: The professor's guide to integrating writing, critical thinking, and active learning in the classroom* (2nd ed.). San Francisco, CA: Jossey-Bass.

Hoy, W. K., & Forsyth, P. (1986). *Effective supervision: Theory into practice.* New York, NY: Random House.

Mills, G. E. (2014). *Action research: A guide for the teacher researcher* (5th ed.). New York, NY: Pearson.

Roberts, T., & Billings, L. (2012). *Teaching critical thinking: Using seminars for 21st century literacy.* Larchmont, NY: Eye-on-Education.

6

✠

Examining What's Known

Educational theories abound in the minds of new and nearly new teachers. College classes inundate these scholars with the latest theories and practices as well as the tried-and-true educational theories. Experience is all they lack as they enter the classroom. Experience, however, is not transferable.

All aspects of teaching are in the realm of new for new and nearly new teachers. Elementary teachers, privileged to teach self-contained classes, will get to know twenty-five to thirty students in one class. Middle school and high school teachers generally meet one-hundred to one-hundred-fifty students a day. Getting to know students challenges even veteran teachers.

The classroom teacher is the best on-site researcher, gathering data daily and determining what works and what does not work in this class with these students. Teacher researchers seek to understand the background of their students. With student information at hand, the teacher researcher examines what seems obvious as a basis for beginning steps to improving teaching and learning. This chapter considers ways teachers examine what they know about the students they teach.

WHAT TEACHERS KNOW ABOUT THEIR PRACTICE

Teacher candidates have two areas of study: education and their content discipline. In education courses, teacher candidates study curriculum, pedagogy, learner development, and teacher responsibilities. In their discipline, teachers study facts and concepts, theorists and studies, and content documents and discourse. New teachers combine the learning in both disciplines and arrive in front of twenty-five to thirty students armed to impart their knowledge. Very quickly the realization that "there is more to this teaching thing than meets the eye" is obvious to the new teacher.

Common first-year teacher questions include: Why don't they listen? What don't they get? Why don't they learn? None of these questions relates to the content that teachers have been well prepared to teach. Rather these questions reflect the experience they do not have.

First-year teachers can quote theories on classroom management. They can explain every step of the well-developed lesson plan. They know ways to differentiate content, resources, and assessments. But as Danielson (2013) relates:

> Teachers don't teach content in the abstract; they teach it to students. In order to ensure student learning, therefore, teachers must know not only their content and its related pedagogy but also the students to whom they wish to teach that content. In ensuring student learning, teachers must appreciate what recent research in cognitive psychology has confirmed, namely, that students learn through active intellectual engagement with content. (p. 13)

New and nearly new teachers, while well equipped in content and pedagogy, have the greatest challenge in learning about the students they teach. Knowing one's students goes beyond knowing student names and interests. Each student has certain developmental characteristics, preferred learning styles, as well as social and emotional background experiences. To address the needs of students, teachers must have a solid understanding of the intellectual, social, and emotional stages of the learner to address the academic needs of students.

Knowing students is multifaceted. Teachers must present material in a way that relates to the students' prior knowledge and experiences, including their social and cultural characteristics. These characteristics influence how students interpret events and how they participate in the lessons. Skilled teachers help students build on strengths and interests while developing all areas of competence (Danielson, 2013).

WHAT IS TEACHER COMPETENCE?

When teacher candidates graduate with a teaching degree and are certified by the state to begin teaching, what competencies do they bring with them? Teachers are qualified to teach. They successfully complete a teacher education program, meeting the requirements of the institution. They meet state requirements for certification, which often include passing a series of state assessments and completing a student teaching experience of a few months to a year under the supervision of a qualified master teacher. What they lack are experience and the competencies related to experience.

In 2001 Singapore's Ministry of Education (MOE) overhauled its teacher evaluation system and researched the competencies that distinguish top-performing teachers. Competency, as used by Singapore's MOE, refers specifically to "the underlying traits and habits—patterns of thinking, feeling, acting, or speaking—that cause a person to be successful in a specific job or role" (Steiner, 2010, p. 8). Interestingly, Singapore used a model that was developed in the United States by David McClelland (1998), a Harvard University researcher. His model is fairly simple:

> Researchers select two groups of current job holders, one that has displayed average performance according to an agreed-upon set of outcome measures, and another that has displayed outstanding performance on the same set of measures. Researchers then use a structured interview technique, called the Behavior Event Interview (BEI), to elicit detailed stories that reveal how very high performers differ from more typical or lower-performing job holders. (Steiner, 2010, p. 8)

The Singapore model consists of one core competency: nurturing the whole child. The details tell how the teacher nurtures the whole child.

All teachers in the Singapore model share values with students and take action to develop them. Master teachers act consistently in the students' best interest, get other educators and constituencies to join the education process, and influence policies, procedures, and programs (Sclafani, 2008).

HOW DO TEACHERS GET TO KNOW STUDENTS?

New and nearly new teachers have to get to know their students. One aspect of teacher training that is lacking is the opportunity to work extensively with students. While most teacher education programs incorporate hours in the field and student teaching for developing teacher expertise, working with students in these experiences is limited. One student teacher aptly described the experience as "cooking in someone else's kitchen" (personal communication). Working with students in another teacher's classroom is not the same as having responsibility for one's own group of students.

Teachers quickly learn students by name, interests, and academic performance. This surface level of knowing is a first step in acquiring knowledge about the students. In her study of graduate students' perspectives on effective teaching, Hill (2014) found that their perspective matched the research literature on effective teaching. In addition to a strong content knowledge, and the pedagogy to present that content, effective teachers form relationships with students and care about students' learning. Hyland (2010) describes learning as developing students' knowledge, values, emotions, understanding, reasoning skills, and insights and experiences.

DEVELOPING STUDENTS IN THE LEARNING PROCESS

To develop the whole child, teachers establish relationships with their students. Bondy and Ross (2008) describe effective teachers as "warm demanders"—they communicate personal warmth and insist that students perform to high levels. They build relationships deliberately, learn about students' cultures, communicate an expectation of success, provide learning supports, and are clear and consistent about expectations. Effective teachers get to know their students through the classroom climate they create, the behavior and management techniques they employ, the student work they require, and the expectations they communicate.

CLASSROOM CLIMATE

Teacher evaluations rely heavily on the academic achievement of students. However, as effective as student scores may be, they do not give the full picture of why students may or may not be successful in a classroom. In his twenty-plus years of research on measuring classroom climate, Fraser (1982) poses important questions for teachers to consider:

- What are the determinants of classroom climate and how do these affect student satisfaction and learning?
- Is there a discrepancy between actual and perceived classroom environments?
- Do teachers and students perceive the classroom in the same way?
- What do teachers "tell" their students by the classroom climate they create?

Fraser describes seven categories for determining classroom climate:

- *Personalization*—opportunities for students to interact with the teacher and the teacher's concern for students' well-being
- *Involvement*—the extent of student active and attentive involvement in class activities and discussions
- *Student cohesiveness*—the extent to which students are helpful and friendly to each other
- *Satisfaction*—the degree to which students enjoy the class

- *Task orientation*—the clarity and organization of class activities
- *Innovation*—the teacher's use of new and unusual class activities, strategies, and assessments
- *Individualization*—the extent students are allowed to make decisions and are treated differently based on preference, ability, and rate of working

Teachers can assess their own classroom climate for each category. However, an outsider's view—the principal, assistant principal, and/or another teacher—is likely to be more objective in observing and recording specific student behaviors and classroom incidents in each of these categories. In addition to the teacher's perspective and the outsider's view, students' perception of the classroom climate can also give insights to determine if there are discrepancies between teacher and students in the same classroom.

Teachers can assess their own perception of classroom climate with the checklist in figure 6.1.

For a more extensive review of classroom climate, Fraser et al.'s (1986) Classroom Climate Inventory is available online at http://www.calvin.edu/admin/provost/teaching/instructional/tools/documents/Classroom ClimateInventory.doc.

The teacher . . .	*The students . . .*
• Greets students as they enter the classroom • Asks students about outside classroom activities (How was your soccer game?) • Speaks eye level to students (such as kneeling to speak at student's desk) • Addresses students by name • Comments on student's response • Invites alternative insights • Gives students choice • Involves all students • Responds to questions • Moves around the room • Is available to all students • Incorporates innovative strategies and tasks • Communicates importance of learning	• Refer to classmates by name • Wait to speak until others have finished • Respectfully correct one another • Offer assistance • Use courtesies (please, thank you, etc.) • Listen attentively to teacher • Listen attentively to classmates • Ask questions • Know exactly what to do in a task • Get to work immediately • Enjoy each other • Work collaboratively • Respect personal space • Take pride in work • Show enthusiasm and interest

Figure 6.1. Classroom Climate Checklists

BEHAVIOR AND MANAGEMENT

Most new teachers struggle with the balance between behavior and classroom management. Harry and Rosemary Wong state, "Effective teachers manage their classrooms. Ineffective teachers discipline their classrooms" (Wong & Wong, 2009, p. 89). Classroom management is a skill that can only be developed in an actual classroom with real students. There are no courses in undergraduate programs that can teach classroom management other than through theory. And while theory is helpful, classroom management calls for a firsthand experience.

Typically teachers develop classroom rules—the dos and the don'ts. Rules are a necessity for creating and maintaining order. But a rule without procedures is really a dare waiting to be challenged.

Classroom teachers envision the ideal give-and-take and flow of the classroom. Safety is a primary consideration. Students (and the teacher) need to be safe—and they need to feel safe.

The physical arrangement of the classroom reflects the age and developmental level of students. In primary classrooms, teachers may have math, science, and reading centers that encircle the classroom. Parts of the room are used for whole-class instruction while other parts are arranged for small-group learning. With older students, the arrangement of desks, tables, and chairs communicates what is important in that room.

Desks arranged in clusters send the message that collaboration is valued. A teacher desk front and center gives students a very different message. Visual display areas including Smart Boards, whiteboards, and demonstration areas allow all students to see and hear, and enable students to participate most effectively. Classroom furniture enhances the learning environment, and excess furniture and clutter should be removed. The physical arrangement of the room communicates to students what is most important in the room. Students' use and misuse of the physical space tell the teacher how the students perceive their place in the space.

Materials are arranged for easy accessibility for all students. Backpacks have a place, manipulatives are stored in appropriate containers, text materials are displayed and easily available, and floor space is kept clear. Students can move freely in the space. Heat, light, and ventilation meet safety codes and make the room comfortable for learners and teachers.

While the physical space is important to enhancing learning, even more important is how students feel in the space. When students feel safe, the brain is more optimized for learning.

Teachers set the tone for the classroom. Effective teachers communicate expectations for students' conduct, and students comply. Classroom rules are posted and reviewed as necessary. Voices are modulated and correspond to the task at hand. When necessary, teachers respond to misbehavior quickly, clearly, and without losing or diminishing dignity.

Classroom procedures are obvious. Procedures are established and practiced. Students know how to enter the classroom, what to do to start the class without reminders from the teacher, how to work with others and by themselves, how to get materials they need, how to communicate their needs to the teacher and their classmates, what to do when absent, and how to respond to emergency situations. The tone of the classroom is relaxed, alert, and businesslike (Jacobs, 2003).

New and nearly new teachers learn about their students in the classroom by observing them in the environment. To test the physical and emotional "safety" of their classrooms, teachers can examine:

- *The Physical Setting*
  - Furniture arrangement
  - Accessibility to learning materials
  - View of display areas—boards and visuals
  - Cleanliness and order of room (floors, bookshelves, work spaces)
  - Physical comfort in the room (ventilation, heat, light)
  - Accessibility of exits and entrances
  - Maintenance of all equipment and materials (scissors stored properly, science equipment used safely, electric sockets available)

- *Emotional Setting*
  - Classroom rules posted
  - Procedures developed and practiced
  - Respectful language used by teacher and students
  - Risk taking encouraged
  - No insults/bullying allowed or tolerated
  - Personal property and space respected
  - Opportunities for retakes (in responses to questions, homework, worksheets)
  - Development and use of appropriate humor
  - Active participation individually and collaboratively by all students

Behavior and management in the classroom contribute to or prevent student learning. Simple changes in classroom procedures can enhance or diminish the learning capacity of students.

STUDENT WORK, VALUE, AND RELEVANCE

Effective teachers have classrooms where students work. After all, teachers have already graduated. If teachers work harder than students, something is wrong (Wong & Wong, 2009).

How students work reveals how they perceive the value and relevance of their learning. In their research on job satisfaction, Rosso, Dekas, and Wrzesniewski (2010) noted that "finding meaning in one's work has been shown to increase motivation, engagement, empowerment, career development, job satisfaction, individual performance and personal fulfillment, and to decrease absenteeism and stress" (p. 93).

The 2013 report by Gallup Inc. found that only 30 percent of the U.S. workforce is engaged in and passionate about their work. The other 70 percent are unengaged or actively disengaged. Gallup defines unengaged workers as those who are "checked out," putting in time but without much energy or passion in working. Actively disengaged workers, meanwhile, act out their unhappiness, taking up more of their managers' time and undermining what their coworkers accomplish.

While this information reports on the U.S. workforce, the information can also describe some U.S. classrooms. What percent of students have checked out? How are disengaged students acting on their unhappiness and wasting valuable time of the students who want to learn? What does student work tell about students and the teacher?

Students' work needs quality from the start, meaning that it begins with the teacher who designs the work for students. Student work generally falls into categories of homework, class work, tests, and other assessments. Ron Berger, the chief program officer of Expeditionary Learning Schools, remarks on the value of students' work:

> In all of my years sitting in classrooms as a student, in public schools that were highly regarded, I never once produced anything that resembled authentic work or had value beyond addressing a class requirement. My time was spent on an academic treadmill of turning in short assignments completed individually as final drafts—worksheets, papers, math problem sets, lab reports—none of which meant much to anyone and none of which resembled the work I have done in the real world. Although I received good grades, I have no work saved from my days in school, because nothing I created was particularly original, important or beautiful. (Berger, 2013, p. 2)

Berger continues with insights about work beyond the classroom as he describes the kind of work students will be expected to produce in real-life settings. Students will be required to produce works of value: e.g., lab reports, medical reports, software applications, web designs—to name a few. If students are not required to produce work of value in school, how will they learn to do this for real in the future?

The value teachers infuse into students' work initiates students valuing their own work. The quality of teachers' design, the collaboration skills in the process, and the precision and perseverance in the process contribute to a work value that gives insight into students' dispositions. The goal is to eradicate the question asked in too many classrooms: "Why do we have to do this?"

In examining students' work, effective teachers consider first and foremost the purpose of the task. What learning will result from this assigned task? How will the learner change as a result of this work? What significance does this work have for making a difference in the life of the learner in and beyond the classroom?

As teachers examine students' homework, worksheets, teacher-made and standardized tests, unit projects, and students' notebooks, the value of the assignment will be reflected in the work submitted by the student. Student work will communicate how students regarded the value of the task, and often, the value and worth of the classroom.

"Once a student creates work of value for an authentic audience beyond the classroom—work that is sophisticated, accurate, important and beautiful—that student is never the same" (Berger, 2013, online). Teachers' selection of work for students that has minimal value will result in minimal engagement. Teachers who examine students' work gain insights into the worker.

EXPECTATIONS—RIGOR AND RESPONSIBILITY

How else does a teacher get to know students? Class records reveal information on students and on their teachers.

Begin with attendance records. A modern proverb says, "Showing up is 80 percent of life" (Doyle, 2012). Showing up reveals a student's commitment and regard for this academic experience. Teachers examine student attendance and truancy records—how many schooldays has the student been present, how often has the student arrived for school on time, how often does the student stay for a full day of school, and what has been the student's pattern over the course of the student's academic life? Attendance best reveals how much a student finds value in "showing up" for an education (Shute & Cooper, 2015).

A second source of information on students can be found in the teacher's record book where grades are recorded. First, study one student at a time. Does the student have a record of completed assignments? Does the student have a record of on-time submission? Beyond assigned work, does the student complete other required tasks, such as submitting permission slips, completely and on time?

Next, examine the class as a whole. Are some assignments completed well by all students? Are there assignments that few students did well—or even completed? Compare these experiences. What enticed an entire class to do well with one requirement and failed to engage them in another? Was it the assignment? Was it other circumstances surrounding the assignment? These records communicate students' response to teacher expectations.

How do students know what is expected of them? Are late assignments or incomplete assignments acceptable? Do students know the expected format for submitting work? Is there consistency from one day to the next and from one task to the next? How would students describe their teacher, and does that description match the teacher's expectation?

> A teacher's beliefs about students' chances of success in school influence the teacher's actions with students, which in turn influence students' achievement. If the teacher believes students can succeed, she tends to behave in ways that help them succeed. If the teacher believes that students cannot succeed, she unwittingly tends to behave in ways that subvert student success or at least do not facilitate student success. This is perhaps one of the most powerful hidden dynamics of teaching because it is typically an unconscious activity. (Marzano, 2007, p. 162)

What a teacher communicates as expectation is one of the most researched aspects of classroom instruction. Marzano notes that this expectation is often not a conscious act on the part of the teacher, but the research indicates that teachers act differently in treatment of high- versus low-expectancy students. Two behaviors communicate teacher expectation: *affective tone* (how a teacher establishes a positive tone in the classroom) and *interactions with students* (Marzano, 2007). See figure 6.2.

Affective Tone		*Interactions with Students*	
High Expectancy Students	Low Expectancy Students	High Expectancy Students	Low Expectancy Students
• more positive • smile more • look students in the eye • lean toward students • friendlier • supportive	• less frequent praise • seats farther from teacher • less friendly • smiles less • uses fewer nonverbal behaviors • less eye contact • less attention and responsiveness	• more willingness to pursue an answer • more frequency of interaction	• less wait time • gives answers or calls on someone else to answer • briefer/less informative feedback • less public feedback • interact less • demand less • make less use of effective but time-consuming instructional methods

Figure 6.2. Teacher Behaviors toward High/Low Expectancy Students
(Marzano, 2007)

While these behaviors are unconscious on the part of the teacher, students recognize different treatments of students. While high-expectancy students thrive and rise to the level of expectation, low-expectancy students continue to respond to low expectation. A consistent level of rigor and high expectation invites all students to reach their highest level of performance.

WHAT DO WE LEARN ABOUT OUR STUDENTS?

Effective teachers get to know their students beyond what students tell them. English teachers teach students how to determine characters through direct and indirect characterization. Direct characterization tells the audience what the personality of the character is. For instance, the student is quiet or the student is humorous (funny). Indirect characterization reveals insights into the character through speech, thoughts, effects on others, actions, and looks.

In the classroom, the teacher learns more about students through these indirect methods: (1) what students say and how they speak; (2) what students think and feel; and (3) how these are revealed; what effect they have on others and how others react to them; what they do; and how they appear.

As this chapter suggests, teachers learn about their students in many ways. Whether students directly or indirectly reveal themselves to teachers, teachers examine the many dimensions of their students that give insights to what may contribute to the problem the teacher has identified. Examining what is known about students is the first step in solving the problem. Without knowing the students, teachers seldom know or can solve the problem.

In chapter 1 of this book, Danica and Jason thought they faced the same problem—students' note taking. Only after they learned about their students—those who were never taught how to take notes, those who knew how to take notes from lecture but not from discussion, students' resistance to note taking, how students used note taking—could they begin to examine what others found who were in similar situations and then devise a plan to meet the needs of their students.

If Danica and Jason did not take the time to "learn" their students, they both could have enacted the same plan but for different problems. Would the same plan have worked? Probably not, and then the problem might just persist and student learning might suffer. Knowing students and what makes their situations unique contributes valuable data in solving classroom challenges.

REFERENCES

Berger, R. (2013). Deeper learning: Highlighting student work. *Edutopia.* Available at http://www.edutopia.org/blog/deeper-learning-student-work-ron-berger.

Bondy, E., & Ross, D. D. (2008). The teacher as warm demander. *Educational Leadership, 66*(1), 54–58.

Daley, A. personal communication, March 21, 2014.

Danielson, C. (2013). *2013 Framework for teaching evaluation instrument.* Princeton, NJ: The Danielson Group.

Doyle, C. C., Mieder, W., & Shapiro, F. R. (Eds.). (2012). *The dictionary of modern proverbs.* New Haven, CT: Yale University Press.

Fraser, B. J. (1982). Differences between student and teacher perceptions of actual and preferred classroom learning environment. *Educational Evaluation and Policy Analysis, 4*(4), 511–519.

Fraser, B. J., Treagust, D. F., & Dennis, N. C. (1986). Classroom climate inventory. Available at http://www.calvin.edu/admin/provost/teaching/instructional/tools/climate.htm. Research describing the development and validation of the instrument appears in *Studies in Higher Education, (11)*1, 1986. The instrument is reprinted with their permission.

Gallup. (2013). *State of the American workplace.* Available at http://www.gallup.com/services/178514/state-american-workplace.aspx.

Hill, L. H. (2014). Graduate students' perspectives on effective teaching. *Adult Learning, 25*(2), 57–65. doi:10.1177/1045159514522433

Hyland, T. (2010). Mindfulness, adult learning and therapeutic education: Integrating the cognitive and affective dimensions of learning. *International Journal of Lifelong Education, 29,* 517–532.

Jacobs, M. A. (2003). *Brain-compatible mathematics strategies* (Doctoral dissertation, Saint Mary's University of Minnesota).

Marzano, R. J. (2007). *The art and science of teaching: A comprehensive framework for effective instruction.* Alexandria, VA: Association for Supervision and Curriculum Development.

McClelland, D. C. (1998). Identifying competencies with behavioral-event interviews. *Psychological Science, 9*(5), 331–339.

Rosso, B. D., Dekas, K. H., & Wrzesniewski, A. (2010). On the meaning of work: A theoretical integration and review. *Research in organizational behavior, 30,* 91–127.

Sclafani, S. (2008). *Rethinking human capital in education: Singapore as a model for teacher development.* Washington, DC: Aspen Institute. ED512422

Shute, J. W., & Cooper, B. S. (2015). Understanding in-school truancy. *Phi Delta Kappan, 96*(6), 38–42.

Steiner, L. (2010). *Using competency-based evaluation to drive teacher excellence: Lessons from Singapore.* Chapel Hill, NC: Public Impact. Available at http://opportunityculture.org/images/stories/singapore_lessons_2010.pdf.

Wong, H. K., & Wong, R. T. (2009). *The first days of school: How to be an effective teacher.* Mountain View, CA: Harry K. Wong Publications.

7

Acquiring New Knowledge through Action Research

Teachers often feel their classroom problems are unique challenges, when in reality this is not the case. Other teachers have the same problems or similar ones. While new teachers bring energy and enthusiasm to their classrooms, they also have specific needs.

> A teacher's first year on the job is often difficult. According to research, student achievement tends to be significantly worse in the classrooms of first-year teachers before rising in teachers' second and third years (Rivkin, Hanushek, & Kain, 2005). The steep learning curve is hard not only on students, but also on the teachers themselves. (Goodwin, 2012, p. 84)

Once the new or nearly new teacher can identify the problem and examine what he or she already knows about the subjects and situations surrounding the problem, the next step is to acquire knowledge by reviewing what others have done with similar problems.

FINDING WHAT THE RESEARCH SAYS

While studying for undergraduate and advanced degrees, teacher candidates read assigned research on effective classroom practices. Once they are in the classroom, this practice of studying educational research often takes a backseat.

Classroom teachers, especially those new to the profession, seldom take time to read research reports. They are often lengthy and technical and are seldom written by actual classroom teachers. A main source of research for new teachers is a colleague who can help solve an immediate problem. Yet the research literature abounds with possibilities for educational problem solving.

Creswell (2008) identifies several reasons for examining the literature on the problem:

- To document how a study adds to the existing literature
- To provide evidence that the study is important
- To build the researcher's skills
- To find models and examples in the literature

However, most of the reasons support the researcher and not the practitioner. For a teacher, action research provides a more focused reason for examining the literature: to learn new ideas and identify practices that improve learning in the classroom (Creswell, 2008, p. 89).

THE PRACTITIONER'S SEARCH FOR WHAT WORKS

Lauren did her student teaching with a biology teacher at West Elm High School. The following semester she returned to the school to volunteer her services to tutor students who had difficulties with biology questions that require a brief explanation in several words or a sentence. Most short-answer questions focus on dissecting a passage or diagram. For example, a question asks which species have the closest common ancestors on a family tree, or what the variable in an experiment is, or why the experiment was conducted improperly. Students take the state assessment at the end of the school year, and these types of questions are part of the exam.

Lauren identified her research problem and worded it as a question: How can I best prepare my students for answering short-answer questions on the state biology exam? She examined students' homework and tests, observing how they worked on similar problems. Lauren studied previous exam questions to note the format of the questions and identify the specific reading and writing skills students needed to answer the questions successfully. She generated a list of key terms pertinent to her study: biology tests, writing short-answer responses, test-taking strategies, and high school characteristics.

Identifying key terms, while an essential skill in reviewing literature, is also one of the most difficult aspects. For novice researchers, finding, reading, and analyzing research studies can be daunting. Joseph Bizup (2008) developed a schema to help undergraduate students understand different functions of research sources. He uses the acronym BEAM to distinguish the different types of resources that contribute to the researcher's literature review:

- *B* stands for *background* sources—the generally accepted and uncontested facts and shared ideas that provide a context for the study.
- *E* stands for *exhibits*, which are actual data, artifacts, and phenomena the researcher considers.
- *A* stands for *argument* sources that are generally the work of other scholars who studied the same or similar questions.
- *M* stands for the *methods* or theory sources that the study may be following or suggesting.

Bizup uses different verbs to distinguish each category: Writers *rely* on background sources, *interpret* or *analyze* exhibits, *engage* arguments, and *imply* or *suggest* methods (Bizup, 2008, 72–86). Bizup's categories correlate with steps teachers should take while using action research in their classrooms for improving students' learning.

USING BIZUP'S SCHEMA FOR ACQUIRING KNOWLEDGE

Lauren used Bizup's schema, considering the background—the facts and ideas about how students respond to short-answer questions. She used information from previous tests taken by students within her school, her district, and her state, noting the types of questions students most often answered correctly.

In reviewing the format of the test, Lauren found that thirty-three questions (one-third of the test) out of a total eighty-five were short-answer questions. To receive a passing score, students had to have a raw score of at least forty. This background information indicated that students had to respond correctly to at least seven short-answer questions to receive a passing score. Seven was the minimum number of correct short-answer questions, assuming that all fifty-two multiple-choice questions were answered correctly. She used this information to begin a plan for helping students with this type of question.

The next form of data, exhibit or evidence information, includes actual data or materials for the study. Exhibit or evidence information varies across disciplines. Where an English or history major may go to the library or Internet to gather evidence, and the scientist goes to a lab setting, the teacher in action research gathers information in the field—the classroom, school, student home environment, or the district. Typical sources of evidence in action research include student work samples (e.g., homework, worksheets, and tests), teacher lesson plans, report cards, attendance records, and class schedules.

Lauren's study included student work samples, homework, and observations of students' work habits. She examined evidence from the state report card on students' performance on biology exams at the state, district, and school levels, and she found that in her district, 3,500 students took the state test in biology, 56 percent passed the test, and 21 percent of limited English proficient students and 53 percent of economically disadvantaged students passed the test.

In comparing this information with her specific school, Lauren found that 342 students took the test in her school, 44 percent passed, and 46 percent of limited English proficient students and 43 percent of economically disadvantaged students passed the test. However, she also noted that 92 percent of the students in her school are limited English proficient, while only 11 percent are limited English proficient in the district.

This evidence gave Lauren another approach to consider for studying the problem that her students had with short-response answers. With more than 90 percent of students with limited English proficiency, Lauren recognized that her students had an added disadvantage when responding to short-answer questions.

Lauren needed argument sources—works of other scholars—that would provide additional insights into students with limited English proficiencies. For argument sources, researchers always go to the library to immerse themselves in the scholarly conversations and findings of those who may have the same issue. Researchers enter keywords in educational databases to search for studies done by other scholars on similar topics.

Lauren added *limited English proficient students* to her keyword search. Based on what she already knew about the types of questions on the state test and how these students approached these questions, Lauren examined what other teachers with this type of problem did. She used the college databases Education Research Complete, ERIC via ProQuest and EBSCOhost, and Google Scholar to begin her search.

Finding studies by other scholars even with access to scholarly databases is difficult. Keyword searches often need adjustment by the researcher. After several attempts at advanced searches with various combinations of key terms, Lauren finally found some studies with the combination of *state-mandated tests, English language learners,* and *writing.*

Novice researchers often become frustrated at the point when their searches do not yield results. Precise and consistent attempts are necessary, because these sources of information are vital and necessary contributions to the study. This review is time-consuming, and using an organized approach to review the found studies will profit the researcher.

STEPS IN REVIEWING ARGUMENT SOURCES

Lauren's search (see figure 7.1) yielded sixteen items narrowed by full-text, peer-reviewed, and scholarly journals. Rarely would the researcher find all sixteen items relevant to the study. A careful and organized review of the studies is necessary—especially when the practitioner is limited with time and resources. These steps can facilitate this process.

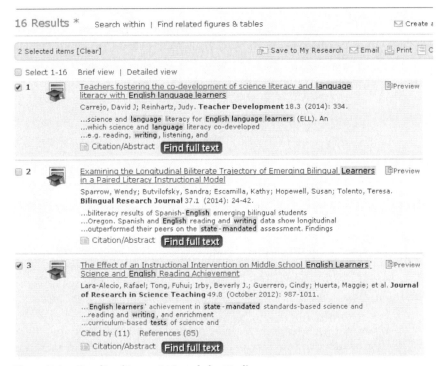

Figure 7.1.   Results of Lauren's Search for Studies

1. *Read the abstract of each item*. The abstract gives a snapshot of the study in 120 words or less. Creswell states that a good abstract contains these key elements:

   - The research problem
   - The research central question or hypothesis
   - The data-collection procedures
   - The findings or results and the significance of the findings or results (Creswell, 2008, p. 287)

   If the abstract of the item matches or is similar to the problem of the study, select the study and find the full text of the study.

2. *Read the entire study.* While the abstract gives an overview of the study, a quick read of the full study provides detailed information on the participants of the study, the methods used to conduct the study, the findings of the study, and suggested next steps from the study. The reviewer can benefit by using these questions as a guide while reading the study: What was the problem the researcher addressed in the study?

   a) Why is the problem important?
   b) Who were the participants/subjects in the study?
   c) What procedures/tools were used in the study?
   d) What did the researcher find?
   e) What are the limitations of the study?
   f) What should come next?

3. *Answer these questions for each study found in the search that supports the problem under consideration.* New researchers often ask how many sources of information are needed when doing a study. The answer is always the same: it depends. Read extensively until the information seems to repeat itself. When studies start to replicate themselves or the researchers begin to overlap so that the studies keep referencing each other, the teacher researcher has probably exhausted the pool of studies.

4. *Read carefully critical parts of the study.* Studies are lengthy and technical when written by researchers and nonteachers. While researchers focus on the discourse of the reported study, teachers want to know what they can learn from the study without having to interpret the research language. For this reason, teacher researchers should read these parts of the research report: the introduction, the study section—including participants, settings, and tools and methods used in the study, findings, limitations, and conclusions.

   While teacher researchers are encouraged to read the whole study, and surely can use data that are presented with percent scores, they can understand and learn from the study without having to interpret the analysis of the data z-scores, one-tailed analysis, and coding of qualitative data. Teacher researchers will learn these skills in research courses in graduate school. For the purposes of acquiring new knowledge from what other researchers have done, reading and taking notes on these sections of the research report are sufficient.

5. *Write an abstract for the notes recorded from the questions.* Immediately following the recording of the responses to the questions, summarize the notes in a 350-word abstract. This practice forces the teacher researcher to synthesize the information just read while the study is still fresh in the teacher researcher's mind. In the process of writing,

the teacher clarifies the ideas presented from the study, and a summary enables the teacher researcher to determine what components of the study contribute to the teacher researcher's study.

This exercise also assists the teacher researcher in determining if any part of the study is unclear and if critical information is missing. Responses to the questions develop the abstract. The complete reference for the article is included as part of the abstract. Teacher researchers should not include extensive quotes within the abstract, as this too often leads to a copy-and-paste methodology that can easily lead to plagiarizing in the final report.

LAUREN'S QUESTION RESPONSES AND ABSTRACT

In her literature review search, Lauren found a study by Carrejo and Reinhartz (2014) on a professional development model used by bilingual teachers of ELLs for developing science concepts with language development. The study, although involving elementary teachers, seemed appropriate for Lauren's study of how to help other ELLs to answer science questions on a state test. The combination of science teachers, ELLs, and language development contributed to Lauren's research question on how to help students develop written responses on science tests.

Lauren first read the abstract the researchers provided. She determined that this study might help her find some strategies that other science teachers used with ELL students in helping them develop language competencies. Lauren read the entire study and wrote responses to the guide questions in note form.

LAUREN'S GUIDE QUESTION RESPONSES

a. *What was the problem the researcher addressed in the study?* The research question guiding this study was: In what ways did a yearlong professional development science program help teachers at ten elementary schools "to become more knowledgeable about fostering science literacy and its role in co-developing language literacy (e.g. reading, writing, listening, and speaking) for ELL?" (p. 334). Teaching science literacy in isolation does not make sense. If teachers can learn how to develop literacy skills while also developing science concepts, both students and teachers benefit.

b. *Why is the problem important?* This is important because ELL students have difficulty with science academic language as well as developing literacy skills for English. If students could develop science and language together, they could be learning more effectively. Teachers who are involved in this study could learn strategies to help these learners, and at the same time benefit from the expertise of each other in this professional development program.

c. *Who were the participants/subjects in the study?* They were thirty-five fifth-grade elementary dual-language teachers who teach science to ELLs; on ten different campuses; yearlong PD program; a district located in a Texas border region; more than 60 percent were Hispanic and bilingual with an average of twelve years of teaching experience. Average class size was twenty-one students; over half the total district population were ELLs and 80 percent were economically disadvantaged.

d. *What tools/procedures were used?* Teachers met for PD monthly at one central location for half the year; the other half of the year they met at their local school to adapt what they learned to their own student population. Science curriculum components included cycles, density, energy, force and motion, organisms and environment; PD model was 5Es—engage, explore, explain, elaborate, and evaluate. The researchers' 5E pedagogy is a modified version of Bybee's 5Es (1997).

QN data included science and reading test scores; QL data; observation of students in the 5Es; and classroom observations of student-to-student and teacher-to-student interactions.

e. *What did the researcher find?* We don't have to teach language before we teach science if we use an inquiry method such as 5Es; concrete materials and visuals are strong supports for developing language as well as science; graphic organizers were good for more advanced ELLs; writing benefited both science and ELA; development of science-based questions required students to use reading, writing, speaking, and listening; no one model of PD, but development of science and language simultaneously will prevent a widening gap for ELLs.

f. *What are the limitations of the study?*—not included in study—but draw these conclusions: nonbilingual teachers; other grade levels; 5Es model; non ELLs; other subjects.

g. *What should come next?*—nonbilingual teacher using the 5E model.

LAUREN'S ABSTRACT OF THE
CARREJO AND REINHARTZ STUDY

Once Lauren answered the seven guide questions, she used that information to create her own abstract of the study. She included the reference information at the beginning of the abstract so she would have the information to include in her reference section in her study. Lauren's abstract is in figure 7.2.

Carrejo, D. J. & Reinhartz, J. (2014). Teachers fostering the co-development of science literacy and language literacy with English language learners. *Teacher Development: An International Journal of Teacher's Professional Development 18*(3), 334–348.

This study examined how a yearlong professional development program assisted thirty-five dual language teachers who taught fifth grade students science incorporate science content and language literacy development. These teachers were in a school district in Texas. More than half the students they taught were ELLs and at least 80 percent were economically disadvantaged. The average class size was twenty-one students. More than 60 percent of the teachers were Hispanic and bilingual, and they had an average of twelve years experience.

The professional development program was for one year. During the first half of the year the teachers met together monthly in a central location; the second half of the year the teachers met in their own schools so they could work together to adapt and plan how to use the strategies learned with their own students.

The professional development sessions included science concept components: cycles, density, energy, force and motion, organisms and environment as was part of the fifth grade science curriculum. Teachers were taught Bybee's 5E approach to teaching science as inquiry: engage, explore, explain, elaborate, and evaluate. The sessions helped teachers study each part of Bybee's model, and learn how reading, writing, listening, and speaking were part of each component.

To determine if the professional development was effective, the researchers collected quantitative data through students' science and language arts test scores. In addition to that data, the researchers observed in the classrooms to note how students worked with each other, and how students and teachers worked together. The main area of focus in the observations was how teachers and students learned science using the 5Es and developed language skills in the process.

The findings in the study showed an increase in students' science and literacy scores within the school year. The researchers concluded that science and literacy do not have to be taught exclusive of each other. Language does not have to be taught before students are taught science. Language can be incorporated into science content and this was evident in this study as teachers used Bybee's 5E model. The researchers also found that for ELLs, concrete materials and visuals were strong supports for developing literacy skills as well as science concepts and skills. They also found that graphic organizers were effective for more advanced ELLs.

They thus concluded that no one model of professional development was necessary. However, they did conclude that the development of science and language simultaneously would prevent a widening gap for ELLs' achievement in science and language.

Because this study included teachers who taught only fifth-graders, the results were limited and could not be generalized to other grade levels. Most of the teachers in this study were bilingual, so the results may not be pertinent to teachers who are not bilingual. This study also focused on science as the major content area and there is no evidence that similar results may result with other content areas.

This study could suggest future studies such as using the same professional development model but with teachers who are not bilingual. This study also suggests that this model may be beneficial for students who are not ELLs. The use of graphic organizers for more advanced ELLs may be beneficial for helping both ELLs and non-ELLs in writing responses to short answer questions in science and other content areas.

Figure 7.2. Lauren's Abstract of Carrejo & Reinhartz (2014) Study

NEXT STEPS IN INCORPORATING
RESEARCH IN ACTION RESEARCH

The teacher researcher reviews each study considered to support the researcher's current study using the same format: thus, read the study with a focus on the introduction, the study components, findings, conclusions, limitations, and recommendations for future studies. While reading, answer the seven guide questions for reading the study. Next, create an abstract of about 350 words to summarize the study and to consider how the study supports or suggests ideas for developing the new study.

The abstracts serve to support ideas for the plan that will be examined in the next chapter. Often new and nearly new teachers need to justify their plans to implement a new idea. The research abstracts can serve this purpose, and the teacher researcher can share the abstract with the administration prior to undertaking the plan as evidence to support the plan. Teacher researchers can also share these abstracts with other teachers and educators.

REFERENCES

Bizup, J. (2008). BEAM: A rhetorical vocabulary for teaching research-based writing. *Rhetoric Review* 27(1), 72–86.

Bybee, R. W. (1997). *Achieving scientific literacy*. Portsmouth, NH: Heinemann.

Carrejo, D. J., & Reinhartz, J. (2014). Teachers fostering the co-development of science literacy and language literacy with English language learners. *Teacher Development: An International Journal of Teacher's Professional Development, 18*(3), 334–348.

Creswell, J. W. (2008). *Educational research: Planning, conducting, and evaluating quantitative and qualitative research*. Upper Saddle River, NJ: Pearson.

Goodwin, B. (2012). Research says: New teachers face three common challenges. *Educational Leadership, 69*(8), 84–85.

Rivkin, S. G., Hanushek, E. A., & Kain, J. F. (2005). Teachers, schools, and academic achievement. *Econometrica, 73*(2), 417–458.

8

Devising Plans for School Improvement
Action Research in Action

Planning is a natural part of life. We plan trips, celebrations, and meals. We use road maps, blueprints, and lists. Thus, plans are used to get from one place to a desired next place.

Even new and nearly new teachers have been a part of planning. For most individuals in this category, the greatest plan was getting to college and then getting out of college. The idea of planning is quite common.

Successful planning is not quite as common. Taking a road trip today involves reliance on the GPS (Global Positioning System). A GPS answers several questions: *Where am I now? Where am I going? When will I get there?* and *What is the best way to go to get there?* These are basically the same questions an administrator or teacher researcher needs to ask when planning to make a change and use action research to improve teaching and learning.

Programs, methods, and instruction in most schools are hardly planned, tested, or implemented in classrooms—for teachers or their students. Often, teachers are "free" to teach what they please, how they please, and when they please—unless they are under review for hiring, rehiring, or tenure.

Rarely do principals, department heads, or grade-level chairs ask teachers in their departments or schools to show them their lesson plans, tests, outcomes, student essays, or favorite classroom activities. But with recent changes and mandates for greater accountability for student learning, school district leaders and school administrators are finally being held responsible to help raise their schools and students to better and higher learning levels.

Take the case of the superintendent in a poor Connecticut school system, Meriden, where former city councillor and mayor and now school superintendent Mark D. Benigni has been able to raise standards and outcomes. As Atkeson (2015) explained:

> But most notably, Mr. Benigni has brought expanded learning time to three of the district's elementary schools, positioning Meriden—a majority-minority district—at the forefront of a national movement to increase student achievement and well-being through longer, more enriching school days. (p. 1)

His planning and implementation have worked. As described:

> Mr. Benigni, 43, has orchestrated initiatives like full-day kindergarten, Saturday enrichment academies, and increased time for teacher collaboration. He has pushed for state-of-the-art learning environments—breaking ground on a $230 million project to build two new high schools, and securing a $3.5 million grant from the Nellie Mae Education Foundation to design student-centered, blended instruction. (Atkeson, 2015, p. 2)

Planning, if done well, can work. This chapter focuses on how administrators and teachers can create a plan that will help them address the problem they have identified and use what they know and what research has shown to be effective in addressing the problem—and thus to promote better teaching and greater student learning. The chapter examines the *D* in *L.E.A.D.E.R.—developing a plan.*

PLANNING IN FULL VIEW

In 2009, President Barack Obama and Secretary of Education Arne Duncan announced a $4.35 billion competitive grant known as Race to the Top to award states and school districts that presented innovative ways to reform educational policies that would lead to greater achievement for all students. To qualify for this grant, states had to submit a plan for reform (Setting the Pace, 2015). States scurried to submit plans that would meet the required criteria.

The plans from some states, such as New York, which was awarded $696,646,000, were approved; the plans from other states, such as New Jersey, which was not among the recipients because of an error in following directions, causing those states to miss the mark for millions of dollars. Accurate planning makes a difference.

Planning and doing a quality program involve six steps as follows. They should be tried and used together, in roughly the following order:

setting goals, determining needs, raising resources, preparing personnel, finalizing plans, and comparing results to other strategies and goals.

The University of Texas, Austin, laid out a three-step process for planning a change in education; these can guide and help school leaders to plan and improve their education process. This model came from Instructional Assessment Resources (IAR, 2011). It involves *planning, data gathering,* and *reporting.*

In this chapter, we take a more active approach, which involves *planning, doing, evaluating, reporting,* and then *adjusting* teaching and learning to the needs of each student. And this model informs us of the steps and background (and research) on the act of planning-implementing-evaluating.

Action research is extensive and points to *PIE—Planning, Implementing,* and *Evaluating,* as the critical steps in the education improvement process, including planning, using former research, data collecting, and letting the world and field hear what we have learned in the process. Education in the United States involves over fifty million children attending K-12 public schools and another 5.1 million in private and religious schools in 2014 with about four million teachers. And costs are about $13.6 billion and rising.

As *Atlantic* magazine states: "Nationwide, 3.7 million schoolteachers serve grades K-12—more than all the doctors, lawyers, and engineers in the country combined" (August 13, 2014, p. 1).

Figure 8.1. PIE. Assessment Process (American Institute for Research, 2014)

This effort is major, critical, widespread, and expensive, with 3.7 million teachers employed by 13,600 public school systems in the fifty states and Washington, DC. Planning and doing well—using effective, good *PIE*—are critical national efforts. The steps in the *PIE* process are important and interrelated, as shown in figure 8.1 (American Institute for Research, 2014).

STEP 1	**Identify the problem or topic**	The literature review will help gain an understanding of the current state of knowledge pertaining to the research idea. It will inform us if the research problem or topic has already been explored (and if a revision or replication is needed), how to design the study, what data collection methods to use, and help make sense of the findings of the study once data analysis is complete.
STEP 2	**Review prior research**	The literature review will help us gain an understanding of the current state of knowledge pertaining to the research idea. It will inform us if the research problem or topic has already been explored (and if a revision or replication is needed), how to design the study, what data collection methods to use, and help make sense of the findings of the study once data analysis is complete.
STEP 3	**Determine the purpose, research questions, or hypotheses**	Identifying a clear purpose helps determine how the research should be conducted, what research design to use, and the research question(s) or hypothesis(es) of the study. Four general purposes for conducting educational research are to explore, describe, predict, or explain.
STEP 4	**Consider research implications**	Implications are the practical ways research will affect the field of education. These are the underlying goals, the rationales for, or the importance of the study. Implications are linked to the research problem or topic, research purpose, and research question(s) or hypothesis(es).
STEP 5	**Construct a research proposal**	The research proposal is a detailed description of how the study will be conducted that includes the title and researchers of the study, statement of the research problem and research purpose, review of relevant literature, research question(s) or hypothesis(es), what information or variables are to be gathered, the participants of the study and potential benefits or risks, the design and procedure for gathering data, what data collection method(s) will be used, and how the data will be analyzed. An example proposal is included in this chapter.
STEP 6	**Gather data**	Data gathering focuses on information acquisition that will attempt to answer the research questions or support the hypotheses. Data gathering includes consideration about what variables to investigate, the unit of analysis or participants of the study (population and sample), human subject protections, procedures used for selecting participants, the methods and procedures used for data collection, and any reliability or validity of collection methods.

Figure 8.2. Steps in the *PIE* Process

STEP 7	Analyze data	Data or statistical analysis will depend on whether we collected quantitative data, qualitative data, or both. For quantitative data, a variety of statistical analysis tools can be used to identify statistical relationships between variables. For qualitative data, data analysis generally involves holistically identifying patterns, categories, and themes.
STEP 8	**Determine findings**	Determine the findings from the data analyses. For quantitative data, we want to determine statistical information and general findings. For qualitative data, we are primarily more interested in detailed and specific findings. If we are using a mixed approach, which we strongly recommend, make sure to triangulate findings or describe how the findings supplement each other and help explain a more complete picture.
STEP 9	**Report conclusions, implications, and limitations**	Conclusions are statements that interpret and evaluate the results found from the study. Be sure to give primary emphasis to the results that relate to the hypotheses or research questions of the study. Factors to consider when reporting conclusions, or data dissemination, include tailoring report content for the audience, explaining the purpose of the study, integrating the findings with the results from prior research, and how the findings relate to the research questions and hypotheses. Be sure to discuss what practical or theoretical implications can be drawn for the study, any major shortcomings or limitations of the research, and directions or suggestions for future research.

Figure 8.2. (*continued*)

The last step is critical—i.e., the analyzing and reporting of the data and outcomes. Without this timely information, schools and teachers may have trouble knowing what's working, how, and when to use it. Figure 8.2 displays the process and dynamics of assessing the results of new plans for teaching and learning in the school and classrooms. This part of action research will be addressed in the next chapter.

STEPS IN CREATING A PLAN AT THE SCHOOL LEVEL

We see the importance of planning in school life for improvement. The process starts and restarts with *Planning*—the *P* in *PIE*. And planning never stops, as school systems set goals and seek to find resources; schools receive these directives and implement them in their schools and classrooms; and grades, attendance, and a sense of efficacy occur right down to the students and classrooms, with the teachers "in charge."

1. Setting Goals

Everyone's somehow involved in planning and setting goals, and the more democratic, exacting, and useful the plans, the better the schools and classrooms operate. Thus, research shows that schools and their leaders (principals and assistant principals) should involve staff in setting their goals and the school's purposes. For as Fitzhugh Dodson explains, "Without goals, and plans to reach them, you are like a ship that has set sail with no destination" (Chandler, 2008, p. 10). Goals and purposes of an education program plan are critical in action research.

As Beverly Swanson (2011) explains,

> To improve the quality of education in the United States, the nation's leaders have established six national goals, based on the premise that every child can learn, and that education is a lifelong process (Executive Office of the President, 1990). Achieving these goals will require the sustained effort of all sectors of society, including business and industry, social agencies, federal, state, and local governments, parents, educators, and the public. (p. 22)

2. Determining Needs

Once school and classroom needs are determined, school programs and plans can be fixed, modified, and implemented. The system, according to research, is "need driven" and requires close attention to the community, classrooms, and curriculum in schools: the 3C's must be *coordinated*, so the *community* supports the *curriculum*, in general; the curriculum is designed for the classes; and school leaders, department chairs, and teachers all generally agree about the purpose and methods of the teaching and use of curriculum.

Every child has special interests, talents, and needs, as do teachers. Thus, teachers must be given support, funds, and help, but must also be given some freedom and discretion to adapt to their students and the demands of the curriculum. One study, done by the European Education Research Association, explained in "Making Policy in the Classroom" (2014):

> We seek to address characteristics of discretion exercised by teachers as they emerge from policies and socio-cultural contexts with a specific focus on (national) curricula or standards and as they emerge from classroom negotiations. Based on Lipsky's (2010) analytical framework street-level bureaucracy the findings provide a fresh bottom up look at teachers' role in

policy making, informs the teaching as professional debate and shows relational aspects of teaching as they are played out in particular social-cultural contexts. (Hohmann, Kelly, Dorf, & Pratt, 2014, p. 1)

3. Raising Resources

Federal, state, local, and school authorities need to work together to raise the funds for new programs and reforms. Thus, planning involves money, and research shows the diversity of resource sources: private and public, national, state, and local programs.

Thus, school leaders and teacher leaders should be aware of, and investigate, sources of resources and place the money where the needs and programs are. Each school needs to decide where the funding will come from and how best to use it. Class size and foci are a major cost factor and should be studied and adjusted for best outcomes.

California leads the way, as "*EdSource*—Highlighting Strategies for Student Success" (2013) explains, for funding and additional help that combined groups of schools, teachers, and community can be involved in while working on school programs. The state encourages schools to identify problems and guides them to additional funding:

> The way California's public education system is funded is changing dramatically as a result of a law signed by Gov. Jerry Brown in July 2013. Its centerpiece is the Local Control Funding Formula [LCFF], designed to send additional funds to districts where Gov. Brown believes "the need and the challenge is greatest." For the first time, the law requires that parents, students, teachers, and other community members be involved in the process of deciding how new funds are spent. The *EdSource* guide provides an explanation of the essential elements of the new system. (p. 1)

Funding programs is critical; without resources, schools, principals, and teachers will often find it difficult to support new programs and ideas. California's leader, governor Jerry Brown (July 1, 2013), explained his and the state's role in supporting school reform and improvement:

> I'm signing a bill that is truly revolutionary. We are bringing government closer to the people, to the classroom where real decisions are made and directing the money where the need and the challenge is greatest. This is a good day for California, it's a good day for school kids, and it's a good day for our future.

He understands the critical importance of school improvements being closer to the people, to the classroom, and where it is most needed. Reform is about our schools, teachers, and classrooms, and most importantly about school kids.

4. Preparing Staff

Staffs particularly classroom teachers, are essential to school planning. We know that, but we have no standard ways of involving them. In high schools, perhaps, policies are often turned over to academic departments and their leaders, who may and do play a critical role in school pedagogy and improved outcomes. Green and Brown (Green, 2014) have done a report, "Building Better Teachers." Elizabeth Green compares teacher review and preparation in the United States to that of Japan and reports:

> Yes, teachers—teachers definitely do not enter the classroom feeling that they're prepared. Most teachers will tell you that their teacher training institution didn't leave them feeling prepared.
>
> And then they do know that they don't have the time and support they need to learn to teach. So, just an example, a group of teachers that I have met with in New York City had a study group, and it wasn't unlike what teachers have in Japan. They have study groups where they are subject-specific, so a bunch of history teachers or a bunch of math teachers will meet and they will share their lesson plans.
>
> But there is one big difference. In Japan, the teachers had sanctioned time in their schedule to go watch each other teach, a crucial piece. In the U.S., when I asked them, do you have any—have you ever seen each other teach, they said—they laughed, like they would never have time to do that. They're doing this in their off-hours. So just the structure of the U.S. education system holds back what teachers know that they need. (Brown, 2014)

One reaction to the report was exciting and insightful online, but was anonymous (2014):

> If you want to attract the best and the brightest to the teaching profession and RETAIN them the entire system will have to be changed. Students who are the best and the brightest are not going to be in a profession where after getting a master's degree your salary will qualify you for public assistance, you won't be able to qualify for a mortgage until you have been on the job 25 years, and the working conditions get worse year after year. As in any profession there are good and bad, the problem here is the really good leave as soon as they can find somewhere better. If you really want to find the WORST teachers, they are often found in the schools of education at the university level.

As Joseph Siudock reported on *PBS NewsHour*, online:

> I see a lot of GREAT teachers become administrators . . . it's really sad. . . . My father taught high school English for most of his life; and I asked him why

he never took the path of administrator . . . he said he loved being with the kids . . . now THAT'S a real teacher. (Brown, 2014)

5. Finalizing Plans Based on the Goals and Resources

In the planning process, efforts should be made to approve the final program, and funds and resources (e.g., staff, space, and time) should and need to be available and allocated.

The cost coverage is critical, and school board, mayors, and other officials should be asked and consulted to gain fiscal support and help. Finding sufficient staffing for schools and programs has changed, as the United States now has more teacher graduates than needs for new teaching staff. Green (2014) explains:

> Yet the United States has, if anything, too many teacher-training programs. Each year, some 1,400 of them indiscriminately churn out twice as many graduates as schools can use. Program quality varies widely, so many would-be teachers don't suit schools' needs. In a scathing 2006 report, Arthur Levine, a former president of Columbia University's Teachers College, accused many education schools of being little more than a "cash cow" for their hosting institution. Among the problems he highlighted were exceedingly "low admission standards," a "curriculum in disarray," and faculties "disconnected" from the realities of the classroom. (Mosle, 2014)

We know that this chapter on planning is the beginning of a far longer, more complex effort to implement, support, sustain, and adjust the change and improvement processes over years. Leslie Asher Blair (2000), in *Strategies for Success: Implementing a Successful School Reform Program,* explained:

> In 1992, based on her work and that of her colleagues, researcher Shirley Hord described six actions a faculty leader may take to foster school change:
>
> - Creating a context conducive to change
> - Developing and communicating a shared vision
> - Planning and providing resources
> - Investing in training and professional development
> - Monitoring and checking progress
> - Continuing to give assistance
>
> These strategies focus on eliminating barriers that can hinder school reform and success. However, implementation of these strategies requires leadership—facilitative leadership—to ensure the strategies are carried out. Consequently the primary burden of the reform effort may lie with the principal and superintendent although others may play important leadership roles throughout the process. (pp. 33–34)

6. Comparing Plans with Others

Finally, schools and school districts are all part of national and regional systems of education and governance (that is local, state, and federal). Leaders of individual schools and districts often ignore this unity, if not centralization. Why not compare staffing, administration, funding, and teaching-and-learning among schools to learn from others and to collaborate in new programs? Unlike businesses, schools can afford to work together and are usually not in competition.

This effort begins with planning cooperatively and comparing the process, starting with common planning and plans. In her review of Green's book (2014), Mosle (2014) notes:

> At the heart of Green's exploration is a powerfully simple idea: that teaching is not some mystical talent but a set of best practices that can be codified and learned through extensive hands-on coaching, self-scrutiny, and collaboration. Yet her account suggests that implementing this vision may entail a bigger transformation than she quite realizes. (para. 5)

DEVISING A PLAN FOR THE CLASSROOM

Up to this point in this chapter, emphasis has been on creating plans for change and improvement at the school level. While this step is critical for improving teaching and learning, most plans will be developed by teacher researchers at the classroom level. The remainder of this chapter focuses on how new and nearly new teachers can develop effective plans for improving teaching and learning.

WRITING A PROPOSAL

In creating a plan for improving teaching and learning, following directives for a plan proposal can be very helpful. The purpose of a proposal is to convince readers that the proposed research is worthwhile and that the researcher has the competence and a viable plan to complete it. A strong and highly developed proposal lays a foundation for successful action research.

Proposals for an action research study should be one to two pages in length. These are the directives we give to undergraduate teacher candidates as they undertake their action research in a pedagogy class that emphasizes reading and writing in the content area. A solid proposal includes the following:

1. Clear Statement of Research Question

Very clearly state what we will be studying. Be sure that this is understandable to someone who doesn't know much about our field of study. If needed, define terms. To test our explanation, give this to a friend not in our major. If he/she doesn't understand, try again! Ask a cooperating teacher or other experienced teacher who teaches the same students if this research question is pertinent for the group.

2. Project Goals and Objectives

Goals and objectives are often confused with each other. They both describe things that a person may want to achieve or attain but in relative terms may mean different things. Both are desired outcomes of work done by a person, but what sets them apart is the time frame, attributes they're set for, and the effect they inflict. Both terms imply the target that one's efforts desire to accomplish.

Example:

- Goal: Our after-school program will help children read better.
- Objective: Our after-school remedial education program will assist fifty children in improving their reading scores by one grade level as demonstrated on standardized reading tests administered after participating in the program for six months.

Note: #1 and #2 are very important—actually the most important parts of the proposal. The rest of the proposal supports these statements. These two components do not need to be long—one short paragraph should be enough—but this paragraph is the most critical. The rest of the proposal will explain why the researcher wants to explore this question, how he or she will do it, and what it means to the researcher and the school.

3. Background/Statement of the Problem/Significance of the Project

Be succinct. Clearly support the statement with documentation and references and include a review of the literature. This section presents and summarizes the problem we intend to solve and the proposed solution to that problem. What is the question that we want to explore in our research and why is this an interesting and important question? In thinking about the significance, try to take the position of an educated newspaper reader. If she or he were to see an article about our research in the paper, how would we explain the importance of our project?

4. Experimental/Project Design

Design and describe a work plan we will follow for this project. Our action research must address using reading and/or writing in our content area to improve student learning. This section of the proposal should explain the details of the proposed plan. How will we go about exploring our research question? What will be our methods? What do we see as a major reading/writing issue we want to explore? (Example: Can explicit vocabulary strategies improve reading comprehension? Will daily journal writing improve students' summary skills? Which reading strategies help students make sense of content?)

Be specific on what we will be doing. The reasoning behind the research opportunity is to make sure that we have a meaningful experience. If the reviewer can't tell what part of a project we will be doing, he/she can't evaluate our experience.

5. Project Timeline

Give an overview of when we are going to do specific steps of our project. This does not need to be a day-to-day list, but depending on the length of our project (our first experience), it may give an overview weekly. Be sure to include time to review/synthesize our data or to reflect on the experience. We should include time to write the final report/paper.

6. Anticipated Results/Final Products and Dissemination

Describe the final product. Our final product will include the publishable manuscript of our action research and our project presentation to the class. This section may also include an interpretation and explanation of results as related to our question; a discussion on or suggestions for further work that may help address the problem we are trying to solve; an analysis of the expected impact of the scholarly or creative work on the audience; or a discussion on any problems that could hinder our creative endeavor.

These directives not only help the teacher researcher write a submitted proposal for the study, but also plan how the study will be undertaken and what results are anticipated. Teacher researchers have had good experiences in planning and carrying out their action research by following these steps in developing their proposal.

A SAMPLE PROPOSAL

Alan, a secondary math educator, worked with students in high school geometry. Alan noted that some of the students had difficulty envisioning geometry problems they had to solve. After observing and working with these students, he proposed a plan for incorporating visual representation in math classes.

Alan's Proposal—A Sample to Follow

While observing in a freshman geometry class, I was not sure what issues I was going to find with the students. However, after watching the students complete word problems during class, I noticed that many students did not draw visuals as a part of their solution. At first, I thought that there was a possibility that the questions were not difficult, so a drawing was not needed. Yet when I looked at the question, I felt that a drawing would have made solving the problem much easier for the students.

After class, I asked one of the students if he made a visual representation for the word problems during class. He told me that for some problems he did not understand some of the words in the problem, so he did not know how to make a visual representation for it. The question became very clear for me then: how am I going to teach these students to create visual representations for their word problems?

Looking back on previous assignments, I had worked with word problems in geometry that required visual representations. Forthmore Prep does not require their students to take the state exams. I am curious to see if the students will be able to not only solve the problems, but also comprehend what the question is asking. Included in my research project, as well as attached to this proposal, are two examples of word problems that the students will use.

A major goal for this project is not only to help students solve word problems but also to provide them with strategies that will help them dissect, comprehend, and visualize what the question is asking. The students will learn strategies that will help them understand the vocabulary used in the word problem and figure out what they are being asked to solve and how to visually represent the problem.

As students progress in the mathematics curriculum, it is crucial they understand certain vocabulary words that pertain to the area they are studying. Specifically to math, many vocabulary words not only provide a definition, but also offer an explanation of how to solve the problem, or a clue of how to create visualization.

After looking at some of the students' tests, I noticed that many were lacking drawings of figures or shapes that pertained to the question. Looking deeper into their responses it became evident that some students did not understand the context of the question, specifically how the vocabulary offered clues on how to solve the problem.

For this project, I will teach them three strategies to help them visualize and solve word problems; however, the students will work on adapting these strategies for themselves. The strategies I will use come from the McLaughlin (2010) textbook used in class.

The first strategy, Context Clues (example/illustration clues) will help them understand key words in the problem. Moving to a strategy that will help the students understand what they are being asked, I adapt the Sketch and Label Connections strategy. This will help the students to begin to think of how a visual representation will look. The final strategy I will teach the students is called Sketch to Stretch. In this strategy the students should have all the information organized to create a visual representation for that question.

Using the key words they found from the first strategy and combining it with their predictions from the second strategy, it will be easier for them in the third strategy to create the representation. While it is important that I teach the students how to create visual representations, it is just as crucial for the students to adapt these strategies to fit how they learn and study. They will be able to differentiate for themselves what aspects of the strategies work best for them.

Timeline

Week 1: Find up to ten different word problems that will be used in guided and independent practice. Also, begin to plan out how to teach the guided practice problems using the three strategies.

Week 2: Students will work on the attached problems before learning the strategies. I will teach the students the three strategies and try one guided problem.

Week 3: Work with the students on three other guided problems; then they work independently.

Week 4: I will give the students the same two problems they solved before learning the strategies. I will also begin to analyze their progress after learning the strategies.

Week 5: I will finish analyzing the data and see how the students adapted the strategies to fit their learning. I will begin to write my paper.

Week 6: I will finish writing my paper and ask my cooperating teacher for any feedback that I can include in my research project.

After going through the strategies and analyzing the problems that I provided so far, I feel that the students will respond well to these new strategies. I believe that these strategies will help them not only understand the material, but also make them feel more comfortable in creating a visual representation to go with their answer.

As a future math teacher, I will be looking for visual representations from my students. These drawings will help me understand if the students comprehend the material. The drawings also help me know where a student went wrong in reading or solving the problem. If the results of this project go well, I hope to continue these strategies in my own classroom. However, even if the results do not come out positive, these strategies are still worth trying, since not every class is the same.

USING THE PROPOSAL

Alan's proposal was his detailed plan for his research. He clearly identified the problem students had in using visualization to help them understand context clues within word problems. He identified the goal of helping these students use visualization and identified three strategies he would teach these students. He gave some background to the problem and the importance of visualization in solving word problems. He made a timeline highlighting what he would do each week to reach his intended goal in the six-week time period he had.

Alan's proposal laid the groundwork for his action research plan. He shared his plan with his teacher mentor as well as the head of the math department. This enabled the teacher mentor to provide Alan with feedback on the plan, and then as he began his plan, to monitor his progression and the students' learning.

The next chapter will address putting the plan in action and gathering data that will help the researcher to determine the effectiveness of the plan as evidenced in student learning.

REFERENCES

Atkeson, S. (2015, February 24). Extra time yields promising results for struggling Conn. schools. *Education Week*. Retrieved from http://leaders.edweek.org/pro file/mark-d-benigni-superintendent-extended-learning-time/.

Blane, G. (2015). Highlights of the state's new teacher evaluation plan. *New York Daily News*, April 2, 2015, 6.

Blair, L. A. (2000). *Strategies for success: Implementing a successful school reform program*. Austin, TX: Southwestern Educational Development Laboratory.

Brown, J. (Host). (2014, September 16). What's the best way to teach teachers? *PBS NewsHour*. [Podcast.] Arlington, VA: PBS. Retrieved from http://www.pbs .org/newshour/bb/whats-best-way-teach-teachers/.

Chandler, L. (2008). *Classroom goal setting.* Retrieved from http://www.lauracand ler.com/books/powerpacks/Previews/ClassroomGoalSettingPreview.pdf.

EdSource. (2014). *School funding undergoes major reform: An essential EdSource guide.* http://edsource.org/wp-content/publications/10-questions.pdf.

Executive Office of the President (1990). *National goals for education.* Washington, D.C. ED 319 143.

Green, E. (2014). *Building a better teacher: How teaching works (and how to teach it to everyone).* New York, NY: Norton.

Governor Brown Signs Historical School Funding Legislation. (2013). Retrieved from https://www.gov.ca.gov/news.Php?id-18123.

Hohmann, U., Kelly, P., Dorf, H., & Pratt, N. (2014). *Making policy in the classroom: Teachers' discretion.* Berlin, Germany: European Education Research Association.

CER 2012, The Need for Educational Research to Champion Freedom, Education and Development for All.

McLaughlin, M. (2010). *Content area reading: Teaching and learning in an age of multiple literacies.* New York, NY: Pearson.

Mosle, S. (2014). Building better teachers: Mastering the craft demands time to collaborate—just what American schools don't provide. [Review of the book *Building a better teacher: How teaching works (and how to teach it to everyone)* by E. Green, August 4, 2014]

Setting the pace: Expanding opportunity for America's students under Race to the Top. (2015). Retrieved at https://www.whitehouse.gov/sites/default/files/docs/settingthepacertreport_3-2414_b.pdf.

Swanson, B. B. (2011). *An Overview of the Six National Education Goals.* ERIC Digest. Rockville Center, MD: ERIC Identifier: ED334714.

9

Executing and Evaluating the Plan

How to Start and Make It Work

In this chapter, we discuss the methods for determining the levels of implementation and the successes and limitations of the plans and programs in the classroom. Without these foci, new teachers may not know and understand just how to do the following: (1) implement their teaching methods; (2) test for effectiveness of their teaching; and (3) see how to improve on instruction. In action research, teachers explore and analyze how well students learn, their levels of involvement and attention, and importantly, how well students score on local and statewide testing in their content areas and basic skills.

For as Goodnough (2008) explains:

> if . . . teaching and learning are to change, then teachers will need opportunities and support to engage in active, ongoing learning that is embedded in the everyday practices of schools. . . . there will need to be more emphasis on "inquiry into teaching," . . . and a new conception of the teacher as one of "producer of knowledge about teaching" and "source and facilitator of change." (p. 16)

TEACHING TEACHERS TO TEACH

What does the research, as applied to teaching, tell us about the preparation and initiating of new teachers into the profession? Helping teachers to learn to teach—and to improve—sounds easy; but it's not. Since all teachers are individuals, with different perspectives, backgrounds, and skills, no single teaching model or skill exists to impart to the next generation of teachers. Each teacher has a unique view, approach, and purpose—which makes teaching interesting and exciting—and difficult to standardize and impart to new teachers.

> Teaching at its most literal level—educating, imparting knowledge—is the most fundamental part of a teacher's job. It is more obvious than (though just as important as) inspiring, motivating and forming relationships. (Teach: Make a Difference, 2012, p. 1)

In part, the training and interning of teachers, when compared to other social and medical service providers, are much shorter, less difficult to enter, and less demanding. And the interning of teachers, often called "student teaching," is shorter and less demanding than the preparation of legal and medical professionals.

DETERMINING HOW LONG TEACHERS NEED TO BECOME GOOD TEACHERS

One of the fascinating debates and issues is how long it takes to train a good teacher. For years, the first two or three years were critical; but recent studies and applied research seem to show that the process goes on for years, for decades, as Stephen Sawchuk explains:

> The notion that teachers improve over their first three or so years in the classroom and plateau thereafter is deeply ingrained in K-12 policy discussions, coming up in debate after debate about pay, professional development, and teacher seniority, among other topics. (2015, para. 1)

Current research suggests the opposite: "But findings from a handful of recently released studies are raising questions about that proposition. In fact, they suggest that the average teacher's ability to boost student achievement increases for at least the first decade of his or her career—and likely longer" (Sawchuk, 2015, para. 2).

DETERMINING TEACHER QUALITY

One of the toughest jobs in education is the evaluation of teachers, to determine those who are quality and should be (a) certified, (b) given a job, (c) given tenure, and (d) even promoted to school or departmental/ grade-level leadership positions in education. In New York State, we learned that:

the Governor, the Commissioner and the Unions spent months crafting a teacher evaluation plan which became State Education Law 3012c. But the plan was neither consistent across the state nor very effective. As a report stated:

The seven hundred plus school districts in the state each created APPR plans pursuant to the law and state regulations and teachers outside of New York City were "judged" for the 2012–2013 school year. (The New York City plan began the following year, the 2013–2014 school year.)

When the dust settled 51% of teachers were rated "highly effective," 40% "effective" and 1% "ineffective." Very, very, very few teachers received consecutive "ineffective" ratings.

In numerous school districts every teacher received "highly effective" ratings on the observation section.

At the same time, the state changed the state tests; under the former tests over 70% of students scored proficient or above, under the new Common Core State Standards-based tests two-thirds of students scored "below proficient," in other words failed the test; however, under the complex formula a new baseline was created. Ed in the Apple, 2015)

THE SCIENCE OF PREPARING SCIENCE TEACHERS

Soprano and Yang (2013) used action research to study the impact of a cooperative-learning field experience and inquiry-based teaching:

This case study reports the effects of a cooperative learning field experience on a pre-service teacher's views of inquiry-based science and her science teaching self-efficacy. Framed by an action research model, this study examined (a) the pre-service teacher's developing understanding of inquiry-based science teaching and learning throughout the planning and implementation phases of the field experience and (b) the pre-service teacher's inquiry-based science teaching self-efficacy beliefs prior to and after the field experience. . . .

The findings revealed that (a) the pre-service teacher's understanding of inquiry-based science teaching and learning was developed and enhanced through the planning and teaching phases of the field experience and (b) the pre-service teacher's science teaching self-efficacy beliefs were improved as a result of a stronger appreciation and understanding of inquiry-based science teaching and learning. (p. 1351)

This valuable research provides guidelines for improving teaching, especially in the sciences for students, based on cooperation among new and old teachers for the benefit of students. As the conclusion states:

Further, the significance of this study suggests the use of cooperative inquiry-based field experiences and pre-service teacher action research by teacher education programs as means to deepening understanding of inquiry-based science instruction and increasing self-efficacy for such teaching. (p. 1351)

Perhaps the best study of teachers and improvement of teaching is in Stigler and Heibert's (1999) *The Teaching Gap: Best Ideas from the World's Teachers for Improving Education in the Classroom.* They found that teaching is cultural and that:

> Using videotaped lessons from dozens of randomly selected eighth-grade classrooms in the United States, Japan, and Germany, the authors reveal the rich, yet unfulfilled promise of American teaching and document exactly how other countries have consistently stayed ahead of us in the rate their children learn. . . . If provided the time they need during the school day for collaborative lesson study and plan building, teachers "will" change the way our students learn. James Stigler and James Hiebert have given us nothing less than a "best practices" for teachers—one that offers proof that how teachers teach is far more important than increased spending, state-of-the-art facilities, mandatory homework, or special education—and a plan for change that educators, teachers, and parents can implement together. (pp. 2–3)

EXECUTING THE PLAN FOR IMPROVEMENT

Just as teachers go through a process of evaluation, so too do they need to execute a plan to make change happen. The development of the proposal, as explained in the previous chapter, is the guide to making the plan work. Part of the plan is setting SMART goals (specific, measurable, attainable, realistic, and time driven). SMART goals can result in SMART plans.

Each part of writing a SMART goal also relates to designing a SMART plan. SMART goals are concise and seemingly simple. They save time and simplify the process of setting measurable goals. Three areas of particular importance in SMART plans are being specific, measurable, and realistic. "The specificity of SMART goals is a great cure for the worst sins of goal setting—ambiguity and irrelevance ('We are going to delight our customers every day in every way!')," Dan and Chip Heath (2010) stated in *Switch: How to Change Things When Change Is Hard.* In writing the proposal, careful consideration needs to be given to the timeline.

Having a sense of how long something will take is not always common sense for preservice and novice teachers. The established timeline will often be the deal breaker in the action research and result in ambiguity and eventually irrelevance. And yet time is of the essence in many classrooms. Teachers do not have unlimited time to make change happen. A SMART plan can make the difference.

CREATING AND EXECUTING A SMART PLAN

Anita was working as a Spanish teacher in a high-performing high school of science. These students went on to Ivy League colleges and even boasted of Nobel Prize winners. These students were bright, competent, but not greatly interested in learning Spanish.

> First language learner (L1) of English and a late second language learner (L2) of Spanish make errors that are considered to be "simple" errors when writing and speaking in Spanish. Most of these errors are concerned with the language's inflectional morphology: how nouns, adjectives, and verbs are modified upon the determiner of the phrase. English has its own system of inflectional morphology. For example, verbs are conjugated depending on the subject of the phrase (e.g. "I run," compared to "She runs.") and nouns are modified depending on the determiner of the phrase (e.g. "a blue trees" is incorrect and should be written as "a blue tree"). However, Spanish has additional elements of inflectional morphology in comparison to English: adjectives are dependent on the noun of the phrase in number and gender. In Spanish, nouns are classified as singular or plural and also as masculine or feminine. In English, nouns are not classified by gender. This is one reason late learners of Spanish have such difficulty with this section of Spanish. They have to explicitly learn the process of noun and adjective agreement in hopes of activating an implicit knowledge that allows us to fluently write and speak in the language. (personal communication)

Anita quickly noticed this issue of noun and adjective agreement was overlooked. Every paper she corrected was covered in red ink. These markings did not signify difficulties with comprehension. It was clear students understood questions or topics when presented in Spanish. Students were able to convey ideas and opinions of the question or topic with sufficient proficiency. However, these writing exercises were inked up because of noun and adjective agreement errors.

Anita recognized that this inattention to detail caused students to appear less literate. Students were in their final level of Spanish classes, and yet they continued to make these all-too-common errors. She had to act quickly in devising and executing a plan that would turn these students around and into competent speakers and writers in the language.

Recognizing their preference for math- and science-based learning, Anita devised a plan to create a practice that made learning Spanish more like math and problem solving than just having the talent or natural ability of learning a new language (which she thought most of these students believed was the case when it came to learning a language). Anita had only seven weeks to work with these students. Timing was critical.

Specific goal	The goal is to have an average of 90 percent of noun and adjective agreement phrases be correct when completing written tasks for all students and to have an average of 70 percent of noun and adjective agreement phrases be correct when completing spoken tasks for all students
Measurable	The original percentages start with an average of 65 percent correct for written phrases for all students and an average of 35 percent correct for spoken phrases for all students.
Attainable	Students were invited to participate in these exercises over a specified period of time. They are open to help so that they will hopefully gain more confidence when implementing the language.
Realistic	Although I aim to improve students' reading comprehension and written work, my ultimate goal is to see if these reading and writing exercises will improve students' speech in the second language
Time-bound	I will meet with students once a week for seven weeks. The first and last weeks I will be evaluating students' proficiency in speech concerning inflectional morphology, and for all weeks I will be developing students proficiency in reading and writing concerning inflectional morphology as well as monitoring their progress.

Figure 9.1.   Anita's *SMART* Goal Plan

Anita used the SMART goal format in designing and executing her plan. See figure 9.1.

The three areas of SMART goal planning made Anita's plan executable: specific, measurable, and realistic.

Anita's goal was clearly understood and articulated. While noun and adjective agreement is only a small part of second language proficiency, Anita considered this an important element for communicating competently. Her goal was explicit and focused. The plan was precise and detailed enough to be followed by other teachers. She set a time limit of seven weeks with a weekly meeting time to practice the exercises she designed. Students were told up-front about the length of this intervention and could choose to commit to this time frame.

Anita had very measurable ways of collecting data. She knew students' baseline performance, and she knew where she wanted them to be within the seven weeks. Students also had this information for themselves and could monitor their own progress. The data were quantifiable, as Anita and her students could count errors before and after each exercise. The plan had the parameters in place that made it possible to carry it out within the given time frame.

EVALUATING THE PLAN USING DATA

Teachers often are overwhelmed with the amount of data required of them. Taking attendance for every class is of itself tedious if a procedure is not in place to do this effectively. Yet the information that is obvious from studying attendance records and other forms of data can be a great help to teachers. Showing up is 80 percent of life; or like the lotto, teachers have to be in it to win it. Attendance data are easy to quantify. One teacher in her action research found that the after-school math tutoring program was helpful to the students who were present for the sessions at least 50 percent of the semester. Attendance in action research studies is a valuable form of data.

Student test scores and assignments are another form of data that help to evaluate the effectiveness of the plan. Test scores are another quantifiable measure that is familiar to most teachers.

Rob assessed the reading fluency of his students. To determine the accuracy and rate of his students, he assessed their *words correct per minute* (wcpm). Each student read aloud from an unpracticed grade-level text for one minute. He noted any errors (e.g., mispronunciations, substitutions, omissions, words read out of order, or words supplied for the student after a three- to five-second pause). He then subtracted the total number of errors from the number of words attempted to determine the student's wcpm. These data were recorded and could be compared to future fluency assessments.

Test item analysis is less frequently used by teachers and yet can be a reliable source of data. Teachers who examine the questions or problems that students answer incorrectly can gather data on students as well as on the questions. As Casey corrected her students' science tests, she noted that the class test average was 75. This was unusual for this particular group. In analyzing the test questions, Casey realized that questions 6 and 13 were answered incorrectly by 80 percent of the class. These data revealed an issue with the content and not necessarily with students' learning.

Another form of data that can be used for evaluating the plan is data from control and experimental groups. Kevin wanted to determine if using specific vocabulary instruction for teaching chemistry would make a difference for students.

Kevin taught his control group chemistry vocabulary in the standard instruction process of word, definition, sentence. His experimental group used a VCEE approach (vocabulary preview, concept outline, example, and evidence) for vocabulary development. Kevin compared students' efficient and correct use of vocabulary and noted which students were in each group. These data helped Kevin evaluate the effectiveness of his vocabulary plan.

Another form of data particularly helpful in evaluating a plan is detailed field notation. A teacher cannot take detailed notes while teaching, but these notes can be taken immediately following a lesson, by viewing the videotaped lesson, or by another observer.

Detailed field notes should include (1) a narrative of what happened in the class, (2) the nature of the activities, (3) the role of students and teacher, (4) questions asked, comments made, classroom climate, flow of the lesson—to name a few. Observational protocols can help teachers decide on what to focus on in the class and how to take the notes (Marshall, 2013; Thomas-Fair, 2007; Jacobs, 2003).

Also particularly valuable for teachers as data are their lesson plans. For all teachers, detailed plans reveal intended outcomes, assessments, and strategies and resources used in the lesson. Of course, teachers need to review the plans they wrote and add notes to clarify what worked and what did not, so they can reference these plans when evaluating their action research or for use in future teaching episodes.

WHAT DO THE DATA REVEAL?

In reviewing data from action research, one can use two or three sources of data to answer the research question. Answer the research question from each data source.

Anita had multiple sources of data—for example, exercises students completed in class, weekly assessments in written tasks, pre- and post-evaluations in speech, student attendance, homework assignments, and class tests. She chose to use the data most closely connected with her research: the exercises completed in class, the weekly written assessment, and the pre- and post speech evaluations.

The other data could also have been used, but because Anita was limited in time and the scope of this research, she used just these data to answer her research question. Mills (2014) suggests these questions for understanding the data: What was learned from the data and what does the learning mean?

Anita's data revealed students' competency levels in speaking and writing before the use of her intervention and after the use of her intervention. The worksheets showed what students were learning as they went through the intervention, common mistakes they made, how Anita's math-designed worksheet gave students practice in noun and adjective agreement.

What Anita concluded from the data was that this worksheet with a math approach did help students improve noun and adjective agreement in both writing and speaking. What she also concluded was that although all students did not reach her anticipated goal of achievement, most students did—and those who did not were only a few points from meeting the target goal. Anita also learned that her worksheet needed an additional column to assist students even further in determining noun and adjective agreement.

OTHER ISSUES TO CONSIDER IN EXECUTING AND EVALUATING THE PLAN

Action research can effectively be used by new and experienced teachers. Keep in mind that the research needs to be a tightly focused study (this is not meant to be a scientific experiment that will alter life forms!), with the main intent to improve learning and teaching in a teacher's class.

With that being said, action research comes under the same legal and ethical requirements set forth for any scientific research that involves human subjects. While the debate continues regarding the extent that action researchers are subject to the Code of Federal Regulations for the Protection of Human Subjects—also known as 45 CFR 46—teachers are held to an even higher code of protecting the rights and well-being of human subjects.

When conducting action research, while a formal internal review board decision may not be required in a school setting, teachers are required to abide by the legal and ethical codes of conduct in their contract. Whenever possible, it is appropriate to seek permission from the school administration for conducting any type of research.

A full disclosure of the research process, the reason for conducting the research, and how the research findings will be shared is advisable. Guaranteeing the anonymity of participants and information that can lead to identifying the participants should be established before the research begins. Informing parents and guardians and students will be the decision of the administration. Whatever the requirements of the school are, they must be followed in all circumstances—especially in using data from a study.

These precautions should not impede teachers from practicing self-reflection, which is a major reason for doing action research. Action research requires a series of commitments. It is a social journey of self through reflective inquiry to improve teaching and self, as well as circumstances and understandings of personal, professional, and political dimensions (Kemmis, 2010, 2011). This "reflection has the potential to lead to significant growth as these thoughtful considerations of . . . teaching and student learning will lay the groundwork for a successful career in education" (Henniger, 2004, p. 369).

Thus, a well-designed assessment system for teaching and teachers is not easy or simple, as the Rhode Island Department of Education (2014) indicates:

> A well-constructed comprehensive assessment system provides continuous, coherent, and high-quality information on student performance that teachers, school leaders, and district and state administrators could use to improve teaching and learning and meet their decision-making needs. At the heart of a comprehensive assessment system is a clear understanding of and alignment to the knowledge and skills and their range of complexity as required by the standards, grade level expectations, and grade span expectations.
>
> These standards should be central to all assessments, instruction, and professional development related to teaching and learning. In a comprehensive assessment system, summative assessments, interim assessments, and formative assessments are utilized in a planned and purposeful manner.
>
> Teachers play an important role in a comprehensive assessment system by assessing student performance, developing and reviewing tasks, scoring them accurately and reliably, developing and employing effective formative assessments to track student knowledge and skills over time, interpreting assessment results, and modifying instruction based on assessment results. Diagnostic assessments or language proficiency assessments are not the focus of this resource. (Rhode Island Department of Education and the National Center for the Improvement of Educational Assessment Inc., 2014, p. 4)

REFERENCES

A. Daley, personal communication, September 23, 2014.

Ed in the Apple. (April 2, 2015). *Olives, condoms, and teacher quality: The Education Transformation Act of 2015 is fatally flawed and counterproductive.* Retrieved from https://mets2006.wordpress.com/tag/nclb/.

Goodnough, K. (2008). Moving science off the "back burner": Meaning making within an action research community of practice. *Journal of Science Teacher Education, 19*(1), 15–39.

Heath, D., & Heath, C. (2010). *How to change things when change is hard.* New York, NY: Broadway Books.

Henniger, M. L. (2004). *The teaching experience: An introduction to reflective practice.* Upper Saddle River, NJ: Pearson.

Jacobs, M. A. (2003). *Brain-compatible mathematics strategies* (Doctoral dissertation, Saint Mary's University of Minnesota).

Kemmis, S. (2010). Research for praxis: Knowing doing. *Pedagogy, Culture & Society, 18*(1), 9–27.

Kemmis, S. (2011). Researching educational praxis: Spectator and participant perspectives. *British Educational Research Journal, 38*(6), 885–905.

Marshall, J. C. (2013). *Succeeding with inquiry in science and math classrooms.* Alexandria, VA: Association of Supervision and Curriculum Development.

Mills, G. E. (2014). *Action research: A guide for the teacher researcher* (5th ed.) Upper Saddle River, NJ: Pearson Education.

Rhode Island Department of Education and the National Center for the Improvement of Educational Assessment Inc. (2014). *Guidance for developing and selecting quality assessments in the elementary classroom.* Providence, RI (RIDE): Rhode Island State Department of Education. http://www.ride.ri.gov/TeachersAdministrators/EducatorEvaluation.aspxhttp://www.ride.ri.gov/TeachersAdministrators/EducatorEvaluation.aspx.

Sawchuk, S. (2015, March 16). New studies find that, for teachers, experience really does matter: Studies cite gains by veterans. *Education Week,* March 16, 1–22.

Soprano, K., & Yang, L. (2013). Inquiring into my science teaching through action research: A case study on one pre-service teacher's inquiry-based science teaching and self-efficacy. *International Journal of Science and Mathematics Education, 11*(6), 1351–1368.

Stigler, J. W., & Heibert, J. (1999). *The teaching gap: Best ideas from the world's teachers for improving education in the classroom.* New York, NY: Simon & Schuster.

Teach: Make a Difference. (2012). http://teach.com/how-to-become-a teacher/get-your-teaching-job. Rossier School of Education: University of Southern California.

Thomas-Fair, U. (2007). *Annotated observations: Field notes and reflections.* Online submission. Retrieved from http://files.eric.ed.gov/fulltext/ED496153.pdf.

10

Repeating the
Steps as Needed

Helping Teachers Implement
Change and Share Findings

A s explained in Mertler's (2009) *Action Research: Teachers as Researchers in the Classroom*, action research is viewed as a cyclical process.

> That is to say, whereas action research has a clear beginning, it does not have a clearly defined endpoint. Ordinarily, teacher-researchers design and implement a project, collect and analyze data in order to monitor and evaluate the project's effectiveness, and then make revisions and improvements to the project for future implementation. (p. 37)

This chapter directs the reader on how to review what has been learned in the action research process, and how to take the next steps in the process. The teacher can use what has been learned to plan next steps for the learner and to share the learning with colleagues.

TWO LEVELS OF LEARNING

In action research the researcher and those who read the research learn two types of lessons: (1) lessons related to the problem addressed in the research and (2) lessons about the research process. In action research, the classroom teacher is the researcher, unlike most research, where the teacher is often studied by outsiders.

While that type of research is profitable and objective, the insights of the participant in the research are often disregarded and not included in the study. With the teacher as the researcher, insights into the problem in the study are more fully developed and contribute to the findings and applications for next steps in the learning and the reflective process.

LEARNING FROM THE RESEARCH PROBLEM

The *L.E.A.D.E.R.* steps in the action research process lead the researcher in a much-prescribed format with its clear beginning for identifying the problem under study. The problem identifies a disconnect among teacher, student, climate, task, and/or formal structure in the learning environment. Once the disconnect is identified, the teacher researcher examines what s/he knows about the background of students, what experiences they have had, how students perceive the learning environment and value learning, and what expectations the teachers have for students.

The next step in the process involves the researcher in finding what other researchers have found through examining studies with similar problems. Based on knowledge about the students and the research from other studies, the teacher researcher devises a proposal and plan of action to address the problem—and then puts the plan in action to address the problem.

Once the plan has been implemented, the teacher researcher now faces the challenge of determining if the problem has been solved. In addition to determining if the problem has been solved, the action researcher decides the next steps with the problem and communicates the findings of the study to the larger educational community.

HAS THE PROBLEM BEEN SOLVED?

New and nearly new teachers who undertake the challenge to solve a classroom problem are actively seeking a solution. The classroom teacher recognizes that the disconnect between teaching and learning has to be resolved if students are to succeed. No teacher is out to fail, and when a problem persists, failures on the part of students and teacher are an uncomfortable reality.

But the counterreality is welcoming. No one will work harder at resolving a classroom problem than the teacher who recognizes the problem. The teacher will be the first to recognize if the problem has been solved or if alternative solutions have to be considered.

QUESTIONS TO CONSIDER

When the plan for resolving the problem in the action research has been implemented, the researcher needs to consider possible next steps. Two questions guide this process: (1) Should the research be continued? or (2) If the research was conducted again, what would the researcher do differently?

Should the Research Be Continued?

In returning to the original question for this part of the research—Was the problem solved?—the answer in the negative would generate a positive answer to the question of continuing the research. The researcher determines the problem has not been solved and must consider viable next steps.

This was the case for Maita, who was working with high school students in an after-school math lab. Students were encouraged to seek math homework help any school day from 3:00 p.m. to 4:00 p.m. Students did not need to schedule an appointment, and a teacher and teacher assistant were available to provide guidance for students in completing homework. After working a few days in the math lab, Maita noted students needed assistance in making sense of the math problem. Her research on what others did to resolve similar math challenges led her to use a graphic to help students map out their thinking about the problem.

Maita originally began using a KWL (what I *Know*, what I *Want* to know, what I *Learned*) chart. She quickly noted that students needed an additional column in the chart to show how they solved the problem. Her new chart was a KWSL chart with each component leaving space for the student to complete the chart while making sense of the problem. Maita worked with the students for ten weeks.

At the end of the ten-week period, Maita reported mixed positive and negative results of her study. On the positive side, students seemed to be more confident in making sense of the problems. Students began to more easily complete the KWSL chart without the prompting of the teacher. Students also showed a more consistent attendance for math lab.

On the negative end of the spectrum, students' learning as measured through assessments did not yield significant improvement, and in some cases did not show any improvement. One of her frequent visitors to the lab failed the assessment on factoring despite that in the lab setting she successfully completed the KWSL charts while working on homework. Maita erroneously concluded that KWSL charts did not help to improve student learning. Maita actually needed to consider continuing with her research and examining the variables that may have impacted this action research.

If the Research Was Conducted Again, What Would the Researcher Do Differently?

Starting over is not what any researcher wants to do. The hours, effort, and planning spent in the research seem a waste of time to the new researcher. And yet what has been learned in the process is invaluable.

Maita recognized aspects of this action research over which she had no control. Her data included an attendance for students in the math lab. Over the ten-week period, approximately nine students visited the math lab. While at first glance this piece of data showed consistency in the number of students attending lab on a weekly basis, Maita had additional insights as she reexamined which students attended the lab. Her data are presented in table 10.1.

Table 10.1. Student Attendance for Math Lab

	Luis	Marcos	Maria	Jose	Felipe	Hannah	Julia	Tess	Melanie
Week 1	II		I			I	I	I	I
Week 2		I		II					I
Week 3	I				I	I		I	
Week 4						II		II	I
Week 5			I		II			I	
Week 6		I				III			I
Week 7	I				I				
Week 8	III				I	I		I	I
Week 9					I			II	I
Week 10	II	I			I	II		II	I

Note: I = number of times student attended math lab during the week.

Once Maita graphically viewed these results, she immediately discovered other information. She found that Luis, Felipe, Hannah, Tess, and Melanie were regular attendees at the math lab. She also noted that certain weeks had greater student attendance. One other observation she made was that while Melanie was a regular attendee, she never attended more than one day a week, whereas Luis, Hannah, and Tess—also regular attendees—had more frequent visits within a week.

These data led Maita in other directions regarding her research. While Maita originally concluded that the KWSL chart was ineffective in helping students, she now considered the impact that attendance had on students' use of the KWSL chart.

If students only used the chart one or two times in the math lab sessions before taking an assessment, was that sufficient practice to master the use of the chart? Should she more closely examine student assessment results and compare those who had more frequent practice with the chart with those who had limited or no practice with the chart? What would happen if the chart was introduced and used within the regular class session and also used in math lab? These questions helped Maita realize that these variables may have a definite impact on the results of the study.

RECOGNIZING VARIABLES OF THE STUDY

Before drawing any conclusions about the study, Maita realized she had to consider the variables in the study and how the variables affected drawing conclusions that could be generalized for other populations. Maita created a list of variables that were critical to this study.

Attendance in math lab was a definite variable. Math lab was not a requirement for these students. Not only was math lab optional, but when students attended and the frequency of the attendance was also optional. One other variable was the tutor the student had in the math lab. Students did not necessarily have the same tutor each time they attended math lab.

Also variable was the math topic of the week. Maita noticed that weeks one, eight, and ten had more frequent attendees in math lab than other weeks. Could that be related to the math topic under study for the week? Were these the weeks in which students were preparing for a math assessment?

One other variable in this study was the use of the KWSL chart. While this was the original focus of the study, Maita could not justify the results of its effectiveness for these students. While Maita committed to using the chart when she helped students in the lab, she was not able to determine how frequently and consistently other tutors in the lab used the chart with the students. She also could not determine if students used the chart at other times to help them make sense of the math problem.

DETERMINING LIMITATIONS OF THE STUDY

Before presenting the findings of the study to other audiences, the researcher considers the limitations of the study. Creswell (2008) describes limitations as "potential weaknesses or problems with the study identified by the researcher . . . they often relate to inadequate measures of variables, loss or lack of participants, small sample sizes, errors in measurement, and other factors typically related to data collection and analysis" (p. 207).

Findings in action research are generally only relevant to the situation of the researcher. With that being said, this does not mean that findings from the study are so limited within the educational field that no one else can benefit from the study. That is definitely not the case.

When considering the limitations of the study, the researcher acknowledges those areas in the study that may cause the study to lack generalizable results. In Maita's study, she recognized and acknowledged that the small number of students in her study and the inconsistent attendance by the participants limited her in concluding the real effectiveness of the KWSL chart.

In the short span of ten weeks, she did not have enough time to work with the same students in implementing the KWSL chart strategy. She was able to note that students who attended the math lab more frequently were becoming more fluent and accurate in completing their homework. As the weeks progressed, she also found that regular attendees (1) required fewer guiding questions in using the KWSL chart and (2) took more initiative with their homework than students who less frequently attended the math lab.

In reporting the findings of her study, Maita moved from concluding that KWSL charts had no positive impact to concluding that the KWSL chart had some positive effects on some students with making meaning of math problems. She also concluded that this research needed to continue, but with definite modifications. She made several suggestions for how this action research could contribute to the field of math learning.

Maita suggested that certain aspects of her action research plan needed to be repeated. She suggested that the KWSL chart be used regularly within the math lab sessions. She also suggested that all tutors in the math lab receive training and practice using the KWSL chart together for a more consistent approach in using the strategy with the students.

Because she could not control when and how often students attended the math lab, Maita suggested that the KWSL chart be introduced and used in regular math classes. This use would give all students an opportunity to learn the strategy and thus allow the math lab to implement the strategy as part of homework help. This strategy would also prevent students from not knowing the strategy and thus using the math lab to learn the strategy. The math lab would allow students to practice with this strategy and benefit from tutors in the lab who could guide students with questions based on the KWSL chart.

Beyond the focus on KWSL charts and their impact for math learners, Maita also suggested a future study on the format of the math lab. One insight Maita gained from the table (table 10.1) was the use of this service within the school. With very few students using the math lab, Maita questioned if a better way existed to make this service available to other students. While this was not the focus of the study, the data from this study revealed the limited number of users.

Maita questioned why so few students would take advantage of this service to assist them in completing homework successfully. While this time and financial commitment on the part of the school provided this service to students, the question remains: Is it worth it? This question may lead to the next proposed study that is simultaneously conducted with the continued research on the impact of KWSL charts in helping students make sense of math problems. The action research cycle continues.

DISSEMINATING THE FINDINGS

Disseminating findings from the study often occurs at the end of the study. Keen and Todres (2007) in their study on disseminating qualitative research findings noted:

> few authors of qualitative studies move beyond the dissemination of their work in the ubiquitous journal article. Though the number of qualitative projects increases year on year, the implications of this work appear to remain on shelves and have little impact on practice, research, policy or citizens. (introduction)

If a problem was important enough to be studied, the findings are important enough to share with others who may have similar problems.

For the practitioner in the classroom, finding the time to write a scholarly article and then locate and submit the article for review by other researchers—who may not see the relevance of the problem or who are looking for the highly developed, statistical-filled journal article—is not practical. The "ubiquitous journal article" is not the only way to share research findings. Keen and Tordes (2007) identified three successful dissemination strategies:

a) Tailor the approach to the audience in terms of content, message, and medium
b) Pay attention to the source of the message
c) Provide for active discussion of the findings

AUDIENCE AWARENESS IN SHARING FINDINGS

The action researcher needs to consider the audiences that care about this problem and the findings from the study. Internal audiences would include those directly involved with the study and the participants in the study. This group would be within the school.

Most likely the first audience will be the immediate supervisor of the new and nearly new teacher. This person may be the researcher's mentor, department chairperson, or an assistant principal. This is the person(s) with whom the action researcher first discussed the problem and the proposed plan. If the problem is a shared problem among several teachers, the community of researchers will be the first audience.

Beyond the first audience level, other audiences should be considered. The school administration should be the next audience level, as the research and findings will be disseminated to other members of the immediate school community. School administrators should receive regular updates on the study throughout the process. Updates can be in the form of e-mails, memos, and meetings but should always be recorded in a written format for future reference.

Other school personnel may be the next audience, including teachers of the same content area or grade level, professional learning communities within the school, and the entire school faculty if the problem affects others in the school. Specialized school personnel such as the guidance department, the school medical staff, and support staff may also benefit from the results of the study.

Often major recipients of the results of the study would be parents and guardians. While this may not always be the case, many problems and findings do relate to settings beyond the walls of the classroom, and the findings can be beneficial to the parents and guardians of the students.

The findings from action research should be made public and shared beyond the school community to contribute to the practice of the field. Groups beyond the immediate school community can include professional learning communities, the school district, the state education department, and various national professional organizations.

MEDIUM FOR SHARING FINDINGS

The medium the action researcher chooses to present findings will depend on the audience. When the findings of a study are shared within the school community where the study was conducted, all components of the study are contained and retained by the researcher. The elements that the researcher chooses to share with the selected audience will depend on how the findings will be used by the audience.

The findings from the study should be shared more extensively with faculty and school staff who may more immediately use the data. If the problem was an issue that affects student learning in more than one classroom or with more than one teacher, the detailed sharing of methods and data collection and analysis will be more extensive.

For other teachers within the school who may want to use the methods in the study, the details of procedures and instruments may be very helpful. The data collected and analyzed may give insights to other teachers for replicating the study with another class, or for making adjustments to the teaching and learning process within their own classrooms or with the students who participated in the study.

While all the details of the study may be of great interest to other teachers, many of the findings will be of less interest to other staff members who may be more interested in the results and what actions will be taken to improve student learning. An overview of results and next steps can be presented in a formal presentation during a faculty meeting.

In sharing the findings with other constituents—such as parents and guardians, board members, and school benefactors—the confidentiality of data must be guarded. Presentations made to these groups may include a PowerPoint presentation, providing an overview of the study with general results from the study, and more clearly developed action steps which will be taken as a result of the findings from the study. Most times this audience level wants to know the answer to the question "*So what?*" Providing the "why and how" of what will happen as a result of the study is generally sufficient for this audience.

Sharing the results and findings of the study beyond the immediate school community generally requires different media. Educators who voluntarily meet to focus on student learning are sometimes called professional learning communities.

> Professional learning communities tend to serve two broad purposes: (1) improving the skills and knowledge of educators through collaborative study, expertise exchange, and professional dialogue, and (2) improving the educational aspirations, achievement, and attainment of students through stronger leadership and teaching. Professional learning communities often function as a form of action research—i.e., as a way to continually question, reevaluate, refine, and improve teaching strategies and knowledge. (Professional learning community, 2015)

Sharing findings from an action research study—by an individual teacher or group of teachers with members of a professional learning community—expands the learning community and thus allows more teachers to benefit from the study. See figure 10.1. The action researcher decides what to share from the study based on the intended goals of the group. The sharing may take the form of an oral or visual presentation, a written report, and/or an electronic sharing through a blog, wiki, or podcast.

Sharing results of the study at a district or state level is generally done through a more formal medium. A professional letter or report to district or state representatives would most often be the medium, unless the research was part of a focused research initiated at these levels. While district and state boards of education may have some interest in research initiatives at the local level, the focus of action research undertaken by new and nearly new teachers does not often extend to the district or state level. (See figure 10.1.)

Sharing results of action research with the larger education community—beyond the school, district, and state level—may happen informally through popular social media such as LinkedIn, Pinterest, or YouTube. More formalized sharing of action research is made through articles published in educa-

	Audience	Medium for Sharing
Within School	Action researcher's immediate supervisor(s)	• Face to face meetings (throughout the research process) • Proposal • Data collection/analysis (student work, test results, collated surveys, etc.) • Written report • Presentation report (PPT)
	School administration	• Proposal • E-mail/memo interim reports • Final written report synopsis
	School personnel	• Small group meetings with oral presentation • PLC meetings with oral presentation and discussion • Presentation report (PPT)
	Parents/guardians	• Home school meeting presentation (PPT) • School website/newsletter synopsis
Beyond School	Professional learning communities	• PLC meeting sharing and discussion • PLC group blog, wiki, podcast
	School district	• Letter to Superintendent • Letter/memo to Board Members and/or special interest groups • Presentation at BOE meetings
	State Education Department	• Letter to the Commissioner of Education • State DOE communication medium—Public Broadcasting, Twitter, Facebook
	National Professional Organizations	• Membership sharing medium—Linkedin, Pinterest, YouTube, etc. • Journal article submission • Poster session
	Research Journals	• Peer Reviewed journal submission
	Action Research Sharing	• http://ccar.wikispaces.com/ • http://www.esri.mmu.ac.uk/carnnew/

Figure 10.1.   Anita's *SMART* Goal Plan

tional literature and refereed journals. While not discounting the importance of this type of professional sharing, new and nearly new teachers often have not had coursework in this type of publishing and would find the process challenging and time-consuming.

Mills (2014) suggested that "99% of articles published (and probably submitted) to refereed journals . . . are by teachers teaching and researching in higher education." He further suggests that "this does not mean it must continue to be that way, and I have been delighted with the teacher research articles published in *Networks*, a journal that seems to live up to its billing as a journal by teachers and for teachers" (pp. 191–192). Other action research journals that may be considered for publishing are *Reflective Practice, Educational Action Research,* and *Action Research International.*

In addition to sharing the action research through journal submissions, networks for sharing action research ideas, results, studies, and other resources exist. The Center for Collaborative Action Research shares through its wikispace, and Collaborative Action Research Network, an international network, shares online and paid membership resources.

POSTER SESSION SHARING

For new and nearly new action researchers, finding the ideal format for presenting their research can be as daunting as taking the first steps in action research. Rowell, Polush, Riel, and Bruewer (2015) describe this involvement:

> Making decisions about involvement in action research carries certain risks. It involves interrogating one's thinking and deciding actively to change established self-perceptions and personal and professional habits to move into the future, recognizing that action researchers are responsible for their decisions and the consequences of these decisions. Specific action research practices are informed by researchers' values that carry hope for the future including the procedural principle of democracy and insights from the most advanced social theories of the day. The action researcher, like all researchers, is expected to share research findings as part of the process of knowledge creation. Action researchers also expect to have those findings scrutinized by other professionals, including professionals whose knowledge and belief systems may vary markedly from those of the action researchers. (para. 5)

One format that is helpful for those who are new to presenting research is the poster format. The purpose of the poster is to display graphically highlights of the action research. Often poster sessions follow a set format known as IMRaD (introduction, methods, results, and discussion). The format of the poster is three or four columns.

Because posters in the social sciences and humanities tend to be text-heavy, the researcher may need to change text to graphics. The poster should include tables, lists, and figures to present data. The poster should use short sentences or phrases bulleted into lists to capture large amounts of information. Persuade the audience by selecting message headings such as *Cornell vs. Harvard in Note Taking* rather than the common nondescript headings such as *introduction, methods, results.*

Select colors purposefully. Text and background colors need to be in contrast for easy reading. Background colors for different sections of your poster should be related. Choose fonts that are easy to read from a distance.

A sans serif font (the kind of font that does not have feet) is a better choice for posters—especially if the audience is three to five feet away from the poster. Arial font has no feet and is cleaner and clearer than serif fonts such as Times New Roman. Font size makes a difference with posters.

Titles should be ninety points or higher and only about six to eight words; headings should be thirty-six to forty-eight points and about three words; and text should be about thirty to thirty-six points. The Cain Project in Engineering and Professional Communication (2003), is one of many resources that provide templates for poster presentations and other helpful directives for creating and presenting posters.

Most posters can be created from PowerPoint templates, an easy way to design a poster because much of the formatting is contained within the poster. Most students are familiar with creating PowerPoint slides, even in undergraduate programs. Selecting a template can be quite easy, and templates are also available in Microsoft Word and Microsoft Publisher. Templates are free downloads at the Microsoft website.

Once the template is downloaded, the researcher determines how the information from the action research should be displayed. A common error among new and nearly new action research presenters is to try to condense an action research paper into a poster template. The researcher should overcome the temptation to copy paragraphs directly from the research paper and paste it into the poster—thus giving a text-heavy appearance to the poster. This is exactly what Kathleen did with her first draft for her poster (figure 10.2).

Kathleen copied entire sections from her action research paper, as is evident in the *abstract and methods* section of her poster. She used paragraphs instead of bullet points and incorporated very limited graphics.

In making revisions to the poster, Kathleen eliminated some paragraphs, converted other paragraphs to bulleted lists, changed the nondescript headings into more persuasive headings, used charts and tables to capture her data, and presented the information in a graphically attractive format that enabled her audience to get the gist of her message with a two-minute glance at her poster. Her revised poster (figure 10.3)

Figure 10.2. Kathleen's Initial Poster Layout.

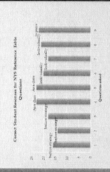

Figure 10.3. Kathleen's Revised Poster Layout.

invites the reader to "see" her research in contrast to reading extensively to learn about the research.

POSTER PRESENTATION

Making the poster is just the first part of the presentation. Presenting the information in the poster is even more important. The goal of a professional poster presentation is clearly and concisely to lead the audience through the study in about five minutes.

Poster presentations are generally held in large conference rooms with ample space for poster displays. Unlike a conference presentation, several posters can be on display simultaneously so the presenter is generally not the only one talking. The audience moves around the room, stopping at posters that interest them.

Presenters have only a few minutes to provide the audience with an overview of the research. The purpose of the poster is to give a visual image of the information that the presenter is making. The presenter should never read from the poster. The presenter knows the research so well that the poster provides the visual for the audience, and the presenter uses the poster to direct the attention of the audience. The poster, however, should be able to stand on its own, so an audience can understand the research even if the presenter is not there.

Think of the presentation as what the researcher would be able to tell someone about the research in a two-minute elevator ride. Stand to the side of the poster to present the information to the audience. Greet the audience, but then give them time to read the poster. Engage them in the research once they have had time to read the poster, or if they ask a question. Speak loudly enough to be heard by all those gathered around the poster and slowly enough not to give a sense of being rushed.

Adhere to the suggested time frame for the presentation. Begin with the major focus for the action research—generally the problem that was addressed. Take the viewers through each part of the research. Use the *L.E.A.D.E.R.* format to present the research. Practice ahead of time and preferably with a real audience who are not familiar with the research. Be prepared to respond to questions, but be honest if you do not know the answer to a question. Thank the audience for coming to the poster presentation.

The above guidelines are formulated for making poster presentations at conferences, but can also be used for making presentations to all audiences. A poster is easy to transport from place to place and requires minimal time to set up. If a poster is designed for multiple audiences, the content of the poster needs to reflect each audience. If the *L.E.A.D.E.R.*

format is followed in the design of the poster, this format can easily be adapted to different audiences with the same effectiveness.

REPEATING THE STEPS AS NEEDED

Action research is never finished. Whether the problem of the research has been solved or not, next steps will need to be taken. Sometimes those steps include revisiting the original problem and determining why a proposed solution did not work. Other times the steps will include moving on to incorporate changes made through the research. In all circumstances, the research needs to be shared with other practitioners who may be facing similar situations in real-life classrooms. If the research stops with the researcher, the learning terminates prematurely. Action research requires action and public dissemination of the findings.

REFERENCES

Cain Project in engineering and professional communication. (2003). Rice University. Retrieved at http://www.owlnet.rice.edu/~cainproj/.

Creswell, J. W. (2008). *Educational research: Planning, conducting, and evaluating quantitative and qualitative research.* Upper Saddle River, NJ: Pearson Education.

Keen, S., & Todres, L. (2007). Strategies for disseminating qualitative research findings: Three exemplars [36 paragraphs]. *Forum Qualitative Sozialforschung/ Forum: Qualitative Social Research, 8*(3), Art. 17, http://nbn-resolving.de/ urn:nbn:de:0114-fqs0703174.

Mertler, C. A. (2009). *Action research: Teachers as researchers in the classroom* (2nd ed.). Thousand Oaks, CA: Sage.

Mills, G. E. (2014). *Action research: A guide for the teacher researcher* (5th ed.) Upper Saddle River, NJ: Pearson Education.

Professional learning community (2015, April 23). In S. Abbott (Ed.), *The glossary of education reform.* Retrieved from http://edglossary.org/professional-learning -community/.

Rowell, L., Polush, E., Riel, M., & Bruewer, A. (2015). *Action researchers' perspectives about the distinguishing characteristics of action research: A Delphi and learning circles mixed-methods study.* Access online at http://www.tandfonline.com/doi/ abs/10.1080/09650792.2014.990987#.VPlW0IH-Oxw.

III

PRACTICAL APPLICATIONS OF ACTION RESEARCH

Part III brings together the steps in the *L.E.A.D.E.R.* process, while giving actual research and examples of teachers and school leaders who have used the steps and methods for action research. Real examples are used to make the application possible. In chapter 11, the whole process is reviewed in an actual action research report. Chapter 12 focuses on the research on research and indications of what works and what pitfalls to avoid.

11

Samples and Examples of Action Research

In his sixty-fifth year, during the summer before his final season as UCLA's basketball coach, John Wooden picked a topic and became a learner again, just as he did from the beginning of his career. Believing that when we are through learning we are through, Wooden provides an image of the teacher researcher who develops continuous learning over time.

> When you improve a little each day, eventually big things occur. . . . Not tomorrow, not the next day, but eventually a big gain is made. Don't look for the big, quick improvement. Seek the small improvement one day at a time. That's the only way it happens—and when it happens it lasts. (Wooden & Jamison, 1997, p. 143)

In this chapter, we provide an actual living account of action research for teachers in the classroom, their administrators who are helping them develop their teaching, and their professors who are teaching teachers how to teach. The example gives evidence of how one teacher used action research in a real classroom.

Carlos, as an undergraduate student in secondary education with a concentration in biology, undertook his first action research project while taking a required course, Reading in the Content Area. As part of this course and under the supervision of a highly qualified classroom teacher, he worked with high school students to address reading issues they had that prevented them from successfully answering multiple-choice questions. He followed the *L.E.A.D.E.R.* format in developing the action research that follows (Perez, 2015).

THE EFFECT OF DURING- AND POST-READING STRATEGIES FOR DEVELOPING UNDERSTANDING IN A HIGH SCHOOL BIOLOGY CLASSROOM

With issues seen in observation experiences in high school biology courses, this research problem focuses on what reading strategies could be used to help students answer multiple-choice and essay questions in assessments. Some of the research has found that concept maps, photos, and more reading-based learning can help students better understand and make connections within biology.

In an all-girls high school, a group of seven girls was invited to participate in a study to research the effectiveness of the semantic map, KWL organizer, and paired questioning strategies in answering assessment questions and overall learning of biology. Students preferred the KWL organizer as a strategy to use in their learning, but all three strategies overall helped students perform better on assessments with multiple-choice and essay questions. The study revealed that students were successful in using reading strategies that helped them learn more effectively and make better connections within the biology classroom.

The Study

While observing many classrooms over the course of my college career, I noticed similar issues reoccurring within classrooms. Many students have a hard time understanding and using the academic language of biology properly in answering assessment questions. Two styles of questions that students have a tough time answering are multiple-choice and essay questions. Although the students understand the vocabulary they read in the textbook, they have a tough time making connections between what they read and what they already know, and to understand other topics that are mentioned in additional readings.

In this study I hoped to find specific reading strategies that could possibly help students make connections within the text to the knowledge they already knew. This study addressed three questions: (a) What is limiting students from using academic language properly? (b) What are some strategies students could use effectively to read and write in biology? and (c) Which strategies work most effectively?

REVIEW OF LITERATURE

Reading as Problem Solving

According to Olshavsky's study (1976), more research on reading and writing strategies is needed for teachers to utilize these strategies. The researcher felt that in "helping students to achieve scientific literacy . . . using these strategies will help schools independently develop better curriculum that supports students' efforts to learn science effectively and more in depth" (p. 656). "Educational researchers, such as the ones in this study, are essential to teachers, teacher educators, administrators, and policy makers" by providing information about developing a curriculum that supports scientific literacy at a higher level of thinking (p. 667).

According to Olshavsky, in a scientific literacy curriculum, reading and writing can serve as dynamic vehicles for learning science meaningfully. The researcher found that the task of educational researchers is to show how reading and writing strategies can be used most effectively to support better instruction and to help students learn effectively within the classroom.

Within the study, Olshavsky found that what is done in schools is based on "teacher intuition—good intuition—but intuition nonetheless, but they need to have more school-based research to validate and build upon these strategies" (p. 667). To further develop his argument, other researchers should try to find specific strategies that can be effectively used within the classroom by teachers to help develop student inquiry skills and learning.

Photographs in Textbooks

In Pozzer and Roth's study (2003), the researchers wanted to look into the importance and relevance of inscriptions (photographs) within high school biology textbooks. The researchers believed that photographs and illustrations provide an element of information learning that texts could not provide on their own, and that not enough research has been shown to support the idea that these inscriptions are essential—just as much as text in the book is needed to teach the concept to students (p. 1090).

The researchers focused mostly on inscriptions that included proper captions that explained what was being illustrated versus illustrations with a brief caption or no caption at all. To study further the phenomenon between photographs and texts, the researchers chose four biology textbooks from Brazil; the textbooks were selected from the same region where they were being taught (Santa Maria, Brazil) and had been written by the same author from the region (p. 1091).

To develop their understanding of the usage of inscriptions in the textbooks, Pozzer and Roth broke down the categories of the kinds of photographs used into four sections/functions: (1) decorative (without a caption); (2) illustrative (describes what the picture is); (3) explanatory (describes the picture and how it relates to the concept mentioned in the text); and (4) complementary (giving new information to the viewer).

The researchers looked at the number of photographs overall in the ecology unit of each textbook and separated the types of inscriptions they saw into their subcategories. They even further categorized the photographs they saw by describing how they were presented within the text (such as placement, if they were appropriately referenced, and number of photographs on a page).

The researchers found that although all four textbooks had similar formats, their "small differentiation between the captions in the photographs and where the index was placed affected how the photograph was perceived" (p. 1096). For some of the textbooks, these small changes caused the photograph to be considered more or less important and relative in relation to the text on the page. Further research should delve into whether these differences had any direct impact on students' learning rather than from just an educated reader's perspective.

Concept Mapping

Schmid and Telaro (1990) wanted to find a strategy that would help students effectively learn the concepts and relationships taught within biology but that would not be time-consuming and only individualized. The researchers found that "biology was an important subject for students to comprehend for their everyday lives . . . but most students were performing poorly in the national exams on average for the biology subject tests" (p. 78).

The researchers decided to implement a concept map strategy within an experimental classroom of level 4 and 5 students at Montreal High School in Quebec and compared the results of the classroom to the results of a classroom with traditional teaching style. The tests implemented in both classrooms included a Stanford Diagnostic Reading Test to test students' readability levels; tests for concept and application learning before, during, and after instruction; and a survey for students to see if they preferred the traditional style of teaching versus the concept map strategy.

In the data, Schmid and Telaro found that lower-level and middle-level learners, on average, performed better within classrooms that implemented the concept map strategy. Higher-level learners, however, "plateaued or even declined in performance within the experimental classroom due to time spent learning and creating the maps, instead of learning the concepts that the teacher could have been teaching" (p. 81).

The limitations of the study included (1) testing that preferred analysis application over actual knowledge acquisition, (2) the learning efficiency of higher-level learners declining when the concept strategy is implemented, and (3) the low reading ability of lower-level students that caused an obstruction while learning the new concept map strategy when initially implemented in the classroom.

The concept map strategy, however, was able "to improve overall student learning while its implementation did not require too much time and effort needed other than learning how to create the maps initially" (p. 82). Further research should be done on the effectiveness of concept mapping in content areas other than biology, the implementation of other strategies that do not include concept mapping, as well as finding strategies that helped lower-level learners learn concepts while still keeping higher-level learners thinking at deeper levels.

Areas of Focus of the Study

Purpose

The research question focused on what reading strategies, both during and after reading, could help students understand the material better to answer multiple-choice and essay-style questions. The purpose of this research was to find appropriate and effective strategies to help students utilize the academic language correctly while explaining or answering questions given to them about the subject matter, in this case, biology.

Participants

To perform this study, I observed a ninth-grade biology classroom at an all-girls school located in a large urban setting. The class included thirty-five ninth-grade girls, four of them with IEPs (individualized education plans).

The students were mostly composed of racial minorities, with Hispanics/Latinos and African-American students predominantly making up the classroom. The students were also mostly composed of middle-class families in terms of socioeconomic backgrounds. They met every day of the week for their seventh period, usually for forty-five minutes, with the exception of Wednesday classes only meeting for forty minutes. The class also met for ninety minutes on Tuesdays for a lab period that took up both their seventh and eighth periods.

Procedures

After observing the class for a couple weeks, I worked with the teacher to develop an after-school study program for those students needing more attention and support in the class and to help them with the state exam. I discussed with the teacher which students in the classroom may need more help with learning the material being taught within the classroom and was able to compile a list of students.

Seven students were invited to join this group. We decided to meet twice a week on Tuesdays and Thursdays for about an hour each day, working on a particular topic the group felt they needed the most help understanding. I used their previous exams on these topics as precursors for their understanding and knowledge within the topic area.

Within the context of the program, I decided to introduce and practice with the students three reading strategies: the semantic map organizer, the KWL organizer, and paired questioning strategy—reading strategies I learned in my course work. For each session we met, I introduced the topic of the day with the semantic map strategy, proceeded to use the KWL organizer, and then ended the session with the paired questioning strategy. At the end of the session, I asked students to describe which strategy they felt was most helpful to them that day during the session and why it was helpful.

Toward the end of my tutoring program, I handed the students a supplemental exam their teacher created using the same questions they had originally seen on previous exams, focusing on the topics that were discussed in the tutoring sessions. I hoped that one of the strategies could be utilized to help answer multiple-choice and essay questions.

Data Collection

Examples of Student Work

Examples of student work from the tutoring sessions follow in the next few pages. In figure 11.1, the semantic map strategy is shown, using work from one of the students in the classroom. The students had to state what their central topic was for the day and then find the links between that topic using subheadings of the map that they created. As we discussed each subheading, lists and points were made by the students to emphasize the importance of each, such as the body systems shown in figure 11.1.

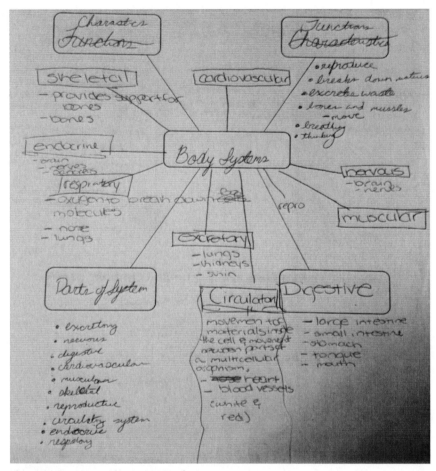

Figure 11.1. Semantic Map on Body Systems

In figure 11.2 an example of the KWL organizer used throughout the after-school study program can be seen completed by Student 2. The organizer was divided into the three different sections (K—What I *Know*; W–What I *Want to Learn*; L–What I *Learned*).

Students first were asked to state generally ideas/points they already learned within the lesson and then write them within the K section of the chart. Afterward, students were asked to write what they wanted to learn more about during the reading, which they wrote under the W section. Finally, students recorded what they learned from the reading and the overall topic, and shared it in oral summaries with the class.

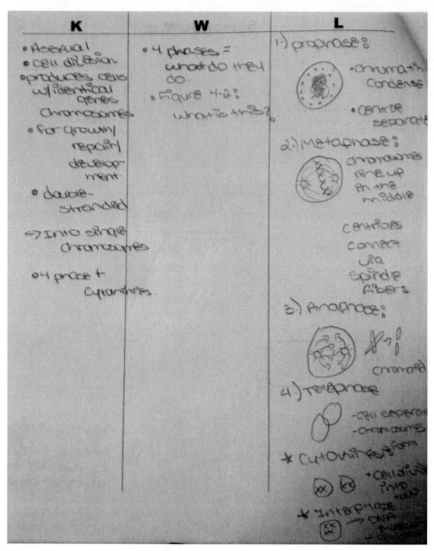

Figure 11.2. KWL Note Taking Example

Figure 11.3 depicts the paired questioning strategy utilized in the tutoring program. Students were asked to create their own questions from the lesson that they learned that day, along with writing the answer for themselves. They then asked their partner the question to answer, and their partner asked them a question. This exercise encouraged students to be creative with their questions, along with thinking critically while creating and answering these questions.

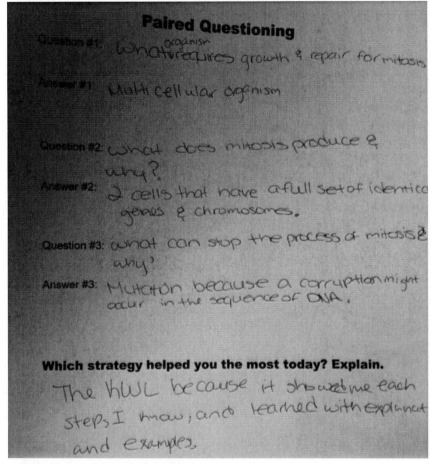

Paired Questioning

Question #1: What requires growth & repair for mitosis

Answer #1: Multi cellular organism

Question #2: What does mitosis produce & why?

Answer #2: 2 cells that have a full set of identical genes & chromosomes.

Question #3: What can stop the process of mitosis & why?

Answer #3: Mutation because a corruption might occur in the sequence of DNA.

Which strategy helped you the most today? Explain.

The KWL because it showed me each steps I know, and learned with explained and examples

Figure 11.3.   Paired Questioning Example

At the bottom of figure 11.3, one can also see a question posed for the students at the end of the tutoring session. The question asks, "Which strategy helped you the most today? Explain." Students filled these out toward the end of each tutoring session, with answers collected and converted into useful data. Figure 11.4 shows an additional example of a strategy choice question-answer and the student's response.

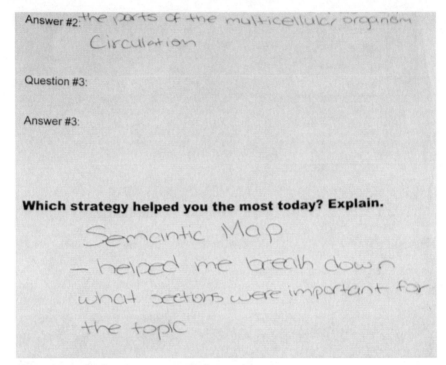

Answer #2: the parts of the multicellular organism
Circulation

Question #3:

Answer #3:

Which strategy helped you the most today? Explain.

Semantic Map
— helped me break down
what sections were important for
the topic

Figure 11.4.   Student Response to Final Question

Attendance

Over the course of the tutoring program, attendance was taken each day to sum up how many students were attending the tutoring program after school. Each tutoring session was different in attendance, with days 1, 2, and 6 having six students attending, day 3 with seven students, day 4 with five students, and day 5 with four students. Taking the average of all six days of data collection as seen in figure 11.5 supports the idea that approximately five or six students attended each session.

Most of the students that were attending the course were returning members, with a group of four students attending every session. Other groups of students came to the session for some of the time or skipped the session entirely and then came to the next session.

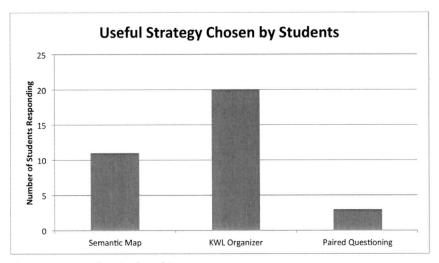

Figure 11.5. **Student Preferred Strategy**

Student Responses

Over the course of the tutoring program, students were asked to choose a strategy that they felt was most effective for them to use during the tutoring session. After each session, the number of students attending the class and the number of responses were collected and tallied.

Figure 11.5 represents the number of times a certain strategy was preferred over the course of the six-day tutoring program. The total number of responses (thirty-four) was calculated and supported by total attendance in each tutoring session over the course of the program. As seen in figure 11.5, the semantic map strategy was preferred eleven times, the KWL organizer was preferred twenty times, and the paired questioning strategy was preferred three times. Students also explained why they preferred the strategy chosen within each session after choosing which strategy they preferred.

Assessment Results

Before beginning the tutoring program, the teacher worked with me to find the average test score each student who attended the session garnered over the course of the year. Once I had the test scores, I asked the teacher to list questions, specifically multiple-choice and essay questions, that she previously gave the students on the topic areas we discussed in the tutoring program (i.e., mitosis, body systems, evolution, and cell membrane).

After the teacher chose the questions, I created a supplemental test similar in style to a test that the teacher gave in the class. The questions were graded with the same number of points that the teacher would have originally given for that question. Table 11.1 shows the student scores before and after tutoring.

Table 11.1.   Test Scores Before and After Tutoring

	Average Grade in Class	*Supplemental Test*
Student 1	68%	75%
Student 2	71%	86%
Student 3	65%	76%
Student 4	69%	73%
Student 5	70%	88%
Student 6	68%	80%

The table depicts the grade average (in percent) for each of the six students in the class based on their tests in the class and the supplemental test.

Table 11.1 shows the average grade from the total average grade students received on their tests throughout the year, compared to the grade they received on the supplemental test provided after the tutoring session. The average grade before the tutoring sessions was 69 percent for these students; the average grade following the tutoring sessions was 80 percent.

Data Analysis

Strategies and Effectiveness

As shown in figure 11.5, students were clearly leaning toward the KWL organizer as an effective tool within the tutoring sessions. Over the course of the six sessions, the students chose the KWL organizer as the most useful strategy twenty times, while the semantic map and paired questioning strategies were chosen eleven and three times, respectively. Many of the KWL organizers were broken down properly and effectively used within the session, as can be seen in figure 11.2, with the appropriate material placed in the columns, and even the use of figures/pictures to help represent the material being taught (in this case the steps of mitosis).

According to the students' testimonials, the KWL organizer was praised for its systematic instruction and its organization of learned material. Student 4 noted, "The KWL . . . showed me each step I know, and [I] learned with explanations and examples" (as can be seen in figure 11.3).

Student 5 also stated that "the KWL . . . helped me recognize what I know and [what I] don't know." Many of the students preferred the use of the KWL organizer during the lesson, as it usually took the most time to complete and kept the students engaged with reading text, learning from instruction, and independent work. Data supported the findings that most students found the KWL organizer the most useful of the three strategies practiced within the tutoring program.

Strategies Helpful in Assessment

Looking at the data presented in table 11.1, I found support that the strategies used within the tutoring sessions helped students relearn and make connections between answering multiple-choice and essay questions. All students had an increase from taking the original exams, with most students averaging between four and eighteen percentage points higher on the supplemental exam that had original questions from previous exams taken.

Student 5 is found to have had the greatest improvement, with an average exam test grade of 70 percent, and an 88 percent on the supplemental exam, a difference almost two letter grades higher. Student 4 had the least improvement, with an average score of 69 percent, and a 73 percent on the supplemental exam. Since the instruction of the tutoring session was the same (first semantic map, then KWL, and ending with paired questioning), one can conclude that the strategies helped students learn the material, or at least review what they were already taught.

In discussing the results of the assessment with the classroom teacher, she was very impressed by the overall better score average of the students. She felt that the students were definitely learning the material better using the strategies and having extra time outside of the classroom to learn one-on-one the topics with which they were having issues. Knowing that these implemented strategies helped student learning can support the idea that these strategies are useful for assessments, such as the state or regular exams within the classroom.

Limitations

Although the data collected support the idea that these strategies were effective in student learning, some considerations of the study need to be addressed. For one, the group of students with whom I worked was not constantly at the tutoring sessions, and their attendance fluctuated every week. Some students were able to make it to all of the sessions, while others needed to leave for personal or extracurricular reasons.

The students who stayed the whole time and attended every session had a better chance of answering questions on those topics versus students who were not attending the sessions regularly. The small population of students attending the tutoring sessions could also make the data collected insignificant, since it was from a small pool and data were collected in such a short period.

Another limitation that should be addressed was how the preassessment and supplemental assessment were chosen. Since I used the average of all the tests/examinations within the course as a precursor for student learning, it is possible that students did well on certain tests but performed poorly on others.

Using these examinations is not necessarily a good preassessment of learning, since some students could have excelled on certain topics over others, so it is unclear where the students actually are in their learning. I also used assessment questions in my supplemental test that were previously asked in other exams. The higher percentages in the scores of this test could just very well be that the students remembered the right answer from the last test where they saw the question. These are some of the limitations and errors to consider within the study.

Conclusion and Future Study

After viewing the limitations and errors, data still suggest that the strategies did have some positive impact within student learning of the topics within the tutoring program. The students did find the KWL organizer to be a useful strategy while reading and learning throughout the session, and even complimented the organizer for its structure and systematic instructions.

The teacher did generally find the students to be understanding the material more within the classroom and reported to me on how they seem to be doing better overall while learning in the class. Although the limitations and errors could have skewed the scores of the assessment, the increase overall for all students shows that the strategies did perform exactly what they were meant to do: help students learn effectively and answer questions.

In a future study, I would like to explore the possibility of using these same strategies on a larger pool of students to see if the same or different results would occur. I would also like to focus more on the effectiveness of the KWL organizer and to look at how to implement the strategy within a classroom setting. I would probably use my own preassessment rather than assessments used in the classroom so that I could have a better idea as to where students are with their learning and have a better chance of getting results that are more accurate.

I am happy to see, however, that my action plan was effective in helping students to learn the material more effectively and had a positive impact on how they performed on multiple-choice and essay questions. Through this action research plan, I can start to implement certain strategies within the classroom and look for signs and feedback from students to see how effective such strategies are within the classroom.

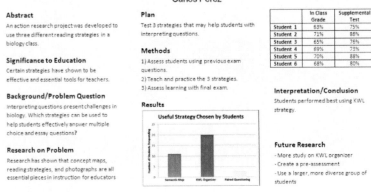

The effect of during and post reading strategies for developing understanding in a high school biology classroom

Carlos Perez

Abstract

An action research project was developed to use three different reading strategies in a biology class.

Significance to Education

Certain strategies have shown to be effective and essential tools for teachers.

Background/Problem Question

Interpreting questions present challenges in biology. Which strategies can be used to help students effectively answer multiple choice and essay questions?

Research on Problem

Research has shown that concept maps, reading strategies, and photographs are all essential pieces in instruction for educators

Plan

Test 3 strategies that may help students with interpreting questions.

Methods

1) Assess students using previous exam questions.

2) Teach and practice the 3 strategies.

3) Assess learning with final exam.

Results

Useful Strategy Chosen by Students

	In Class Grade	Supplemental Test
Student 1	63%	75%
Student 2	71%	86%
Student 3	65%	76%
Student 4	69%	73%
Student 5	70%	88%
Student 6	68%	80%

Interpretation/Conclusion

Students performed best using KWL strategy.

Future Research

- More study on KWL organizer

- Create a pre-assessment

- Use a larger, more diverse group of students

Figure 11.6. Carlos's Poster Presentation

Insights into Carlos's Action Research

Carlos's study is an example of an undergraduate's first attempt at using action research. He followed the six steps of the *L.E.A.D.E.R.* model in developing his study and action plan.

While Carlos was very cognizant of the limitations of his study, he nevertheless was able to bring about learning for his students and himself. He followed Wooden and Jamison's (1997) advice: "Don't look for the big, quick improvement. Seek the small improvement one day at a time" (p. 143).

For the new and nearly new teacher, these steps may seem too small and the results too limited. But it is in taking those small steps that novice teachers become teacher researchers—making a difference one student, one strategy at a time.

REFERENCES

Olshavsky, J. E. (1976). Reading as problem solving: An investigation of strategies. *Reading Research Quarterly*, 654–674.

Perez, C. (2015). *Action research: The effect of during and post reading strategies for developing understanding in a high school biology classroom.* Unpublished manuscript, School of Education and Health, Riverdale, NY: Manhattan College.

Pozzer, L., & Roth, W. M. (2003). Prevalence, function, and structure of photographs in high school biology textbooks. *Journal of Research in Science Teaching*, 40(10), 1089–1114.

Schmid, R. F., & Telaro, G. (1990). Concept mapping as an instructional strategy for high school biology. *Journal of Educational Research, 84*(2), 78–85.

Wooden, J., & Jamison, S. (1997). *Wooden: A lifetime of observations and reflections on and off the court.* Lincolnwood, IL: Contemporary.

12

Research on the Research

*What Works in Action Research
and What Pitfalls to Avoid*

As with all research, action research has possibilities and limitations. While new and nearly new teachers can greatly benefit from the reflective practice of action research, they may lack the experience and objectivity to produce valid and reliable findings.

This final chapter will examine aspects of action research that promote students' learning and teachers' growth. The chapter will also consider the drawbacks that need to be considered and suggest ways to avoid academic and ethical dilemmas in action research.

RESEARCH ON ACTION RESEARCH

To improve and develop teaching, research is needed on what is happening in the classroom. If the teacher does not understand what is happening in the classroom or why it is happening, changes in the classroom may result from a whimsical response to another new theory. While common sense may suggest that the one who is closest to the situation—in this case the classroom teacher—would be the best person to explain what is going on and why, most classroom research is done by outsiders.

This approach is not unrealistic, considering that a classroom teacher does not generally have the time, expertise, and in some cases, even the support of the educational community to conduct research. The classroom teacher with little statistical experience would likely have issues with validity and reliability and the production of new knowledge. While this may be the case for those conducting scientific research, this does not have to be the case (and as studies show, it is not the case) when teachers use action research to study their own practices and their students' learning.

Zambo's (2014) study of seventy-two doctoral research students who used action research methodology for their dissertations found "a blending of practical knowledge with implicit theories and grand theories helped students develop an understanding of their contexts and the actions they needed to take to ensure student learning, teacher efficacy, and organizational development" (p. 505). These students chose a doctoral program that supported action research because the program allowed them to remain in the field as they completed their study in the workplace.

Miriam Giguere (2015) conducted a study comparing the practices of action research with the practices of dance education. She discovered connections in four categories for the two ideas: (1) taking responsibility for teaching outcomes, (2) enhancing self-reflective teaching and curriculum design, (3) giving voice to dance students and teachers, and (4) adding to the body of rigorous dance research. While Giguere focused on dance education, the four connections can be made in all aspects of education.

Lattimer (2012) found that even teacher candidates who were involved with using action research as a part of their preparation program reported that they were more focused on their students, more in control of their practice, and more confident in their teacher voice. Participants reported that action research "empowered them to move beyond the apprenticeship model provided by their cooperating teacher and to leverage their learning to advocate for change in their schools" (p. 20).

Teachers who practice action research find this to be an empowering experience. Action research has a positive impact on the profession and the practitioner for several reasons: (1) the research is always relevant to the participants; (2) the researcher has control over the process; and (3) the teacher researcher makes a difference in what s/he cares about most—student learning and the development of teaching practice (Sagor, 2005).

RELEVANCE TO THE PARTICIPANTS

One of the great criticisms of educational research is that the research is outside the scope of those being researched. In scientific research, it makes sense to be the outside observer taking an objective view of what is happening. The very definition of *scientific method* suggests some definitive directions for a study:

> The principle and empirical processes of discovery and demonstration considered characteristic of or necessary for scientific investigation, generally involving the observation of phenomena, the formulation of a hypothesis

concerning the phenomena, experimentation to demonstrate the truth or falseness of the hypothesis, and a conclusion that validates the hypothesis. (*American Heritage Dictionary*, 2011)

Scientific research carefully controls for variables, observes phenomena under study, experiments, and seeks definitively to prove or disprove a hypothesis. Action research in classrooms and educational settings cannot function in the same way. When it comes to studying the phenomena of the educational process, few proofs work in every situation and setting.

So why bother to embrace action research? For the classroom teacher, the answer is because a problem may need to be solved or be a challenge to undertake. The situation has to do with real life and life today—not tomorrow or in some distant future. The difference the research can make is critical to the teacher researcher and the work done by that teacher, and even to the students being taught.

Educators who choose action research acknowledge the disconnect between the scientific methods learned through the generally acceptable concept of research and the realities of the classroom. Teachers often have their own agenda of action research, consciously or unconsciously. They practice political activity before they enter a classroom; they are community activists who try to right the wronged; and they themselves are influenced by great teachers. Even while taking undergraduate courses, they questioned theories they learned to seek other ways, considered other possibilities, and recognized that knowledge comes from doing.

The challenge that action research is real research continues among the scholars. "Conventional researchers worry about objectivity, distance, and controls. Action researchers worry about relevance, social change, and validity tested in action by the most at-risk stakeholders" (Brydon-Miller, Greenwood, & Maguire, 2003, p. 25). They seek to make a difference where they are. They do that by focusing on their own classrooms and students.

PAYING ATTENTION TO THE DAILY CLASSROOM HAPPENINGS

No one pays more attention to what goes on in a classroom than the teacher. There are several iterations of the saying "What gets measured gets noticed and what gets noticed gets done," and nowhere does this apply more than in the classroom. Measuring outcomes has become the new standard operating procedure in schools today. Quality reviews, school report cards, assessment reports, school improvement plans, school accountability tools, and national report cards—all these documents and reports have to do with measuring and a hope of making it all better.

This system of accountability starts in the classroom. Teachers pay attention to more than just the students whom they teach and the content they teach them. Four areas contribute to the bigger picture when determining what works and what does not in the classroom: students' attendance, performance, behavior, and use of time.

We know that many teachers can and do conduct basic research in their own classrooms—about their own work—to track students' progress and efforts and to figure out what works best for pupils and themselves. And teachers must regularly and systematically keep data on students' attendance (and absences/truancy), tardiness, homework grades, test and essay results—and anything else appropriate for their classes, students' learning levels, activities, and, of course, testing.

Taking and keeping attendance are a part of the job. Keeping accurate records contributes to the knowledge and professionalism of the teacher. Attendance can reveal many happenings in the life of the child and the classroom. Shute and Cooper (2014) explain that truancy is not just about students who don't show up for school. There are several forms of truancy, and one that is common in schools today is "truancy within school"—students who come to school but do not go to class. Where are these students? Studies reveal they are in the bathrooms, the cafeteria, hanging out in hallways and stairwells—reported as present but not in the classroom.

A school nurse asked the principal what was happening in Ms. W's fourth-grade class. The nurse noted that within the month she had 64 percent more fourth-graders in the clinic than the entire school population combined for anything from requesting Band-Aids to complaining of stomachaches. Very few of those visits from that class of fourth-graders merited anything more than attention, but it was getting them out of class. So the question becomes, what needs are not being met in the classroom? And, what does this tell the teacher? Students will not tolerate teachers who are not well prepared and classes that are boring—or both (Shute & Cooper, 2014).

The classroom provides other information for the teacher. For example, among students who are in class, who are the ones who are engaged in learning? How many students not only answer teacher questions but also pose questions to the teacher and their classmates? How do students participate in class discussions and group work? These bits of information tell the teacher (action researcher) what is going on in that classroom and what needs to change.

Another great revelation about the classroom is how time is used. Since the late nineteenth century, the Carnegie Unit—a system developed for awarding academic credit based on how much time students spent in direct contact with the classroom teacher—established that one-hundred-twenty contact hours a year was the norm for high school students. That breakdown meant one hour a day, five days a week, for twenty-four weeks with a total of seventy-two-hundred minutes a year (Carnegie Unit, 2013). Several issues surface when considering this measurement.

How much time is devoted to actual learning in each class session? If class is scheduled to begin at 10:20 a.m. and students are still coming in at 10:25, 10:30, or later, where is the direct contact for those students—and for the students who are present but are distracted by the stragglers who keep showing up? What is a teacher to do with this situation?

Further consideration needs to be given to other interruptions and disruptions that may occur—announcements from the office, fire drills, the student who is asleep in class, the bully. How well is time used—and does learning happen until the end of the class or are students packing up during the last minutes to move on? Just because students are present physically, does that guarantee learning?

These few issues can make or break the quality of education. These are not the issues that most researchers in universities will want to address in a study. But the classroom teacher recognizes that these are the real issues: the everyday situations that make a difference in the life of the learner. The classroom teacher can readily research the impact these issues have on the learners in his or her class. These are issues that matter.

REFLECTIVE PRACTICE

"Practice is not created and developed by individual teachers but is subject to what Kemmis and Grootenboer (2008) called 'extra-individual conditions' and cultural histories. The 'expectations' around teaching do much to create stereotypes and conformity around how to teach and how to act in schools" (Casey, 2012, p. 219). Teachers are "trained" to teach in certain ways, use certain strategies, and mimic their own learning experiences.

Teachers need to reflect on their own practice to improve that practice. This is especially true for new and nearly new teachers who are still under the notion that "someone else will tell me how well I am doing." Having spent years under the directive of teachers who made those decisions— did your paper get an A or B—novice teachers (and in some cases teachers with many years' experiences) need to learn how to make decisions about their educational choices and inquire into their own teaching.

While reflective practice may initially be uncomfortable, contemplation on one's actions gradually informs practice. Incorporating reflective practice in teaching has positive results.

Hagevik, Aydeniz, and Rowell (2012), in their study with twenty pre-service teachers, found that conducting action research as a part of their program (a) engaged them in inquiry into their own practice, (b) was a means to reflect upon and determine ways to change their teaching practices, and (c) promoted critical reflection in a collaborative learning environment. They further suggested that these skills could help promote teacher retention, as the twenty teachers in the study were still in classrooms in their second year in contrast to nearly one-third who ordinarily leave in the first three years.

The practice of reflective teaching is a natural component of action research. When a teacher confronts a problem or challenge, the teacher needs time to determine all the steps associated with action research. Reflective practitioners who steep themselves in the steps of action research often find ways to resolve issues they experienced and frequently learn about themselves and their practice of teaching in the process. Reflection has the potential to lead to significant growth as the study of teaching and learning lays groundwork for a successful career (Ryan, 2013).

Teaching can always be improved at all levels. But "teachers develop gradually via experience and inner-growth" (Ryan, 2013, p. 4). Without reflection, teaching stagnates. Reflection on teaching requires an active and consistent process (action research) that leads to new actions, new thoughts, and new and constant learning.

FINDING THE TEACHER VOICE

Historically, teachers have not always been regarded as an important source of information. While teachers spend more time with students than parents often do, what teachers have to say is rarely recognized, and sadly, often silenced.

When a teacher enters the classroom, a closed door generally follows. While this closed classroom door is meant to keep order for all those in the building, metaphorically the closed door shuts out and keeps within the expertise of one in an ideal position to determine what is best for students. Teachers teach based on how they were taught or by enacting techniques that others have determined to be effective. Action research can contribute to finding the teacher's voice.

In their study of science teachers, Jordan, Perry, and Bevans (2011) stated:

> It is important to recognize and capture the rich and complex knowledge, understanding and experience that comes with the day-to-day interactions of those immersed in the school and science classroom environment, so that policy-makers do not overlook those who practice in the classroom and theorists do not assign incorrect meaning to the actions of classroom teachers. (p. 12)

The Teacher Action Research Cluster (TARC) model serves to give voice to teachers through a collaborative sharing that supports the empowerment of teachers and provides a pathway for connecting theory and practice.

Teachers are agents of action in action research. In an uncharacteristic role of researcher instead of the subject of research, the teacher joins action to research. As Pine (2009) explains:

> Teachers are privileged through the action research process to produce knowledge and consequently experience that 'knowledge is power.' As knowledge and action are joined in changing practice, there is growing recognition of the power of teachers to change and reform education from the inside rather than having change and reform imposed top down from the outside. (p. 31)

While the role of the teacher has changed to encompass the role of researcher, so has the responsibility to share learning from their studies. The teacher's voice needs to be heard in the public arena so that change can happen from the inside out.

Ryan (2013) concludes his study by stating that action research demands a series of commitments.

> It is a journey through reflective inquiry that is social (Kemmis, 2010). We do it to improve our teaching and self. We desire to improve praxes (practices) and understanding within the context in which these understandings are implemented (Kemmis, 2011) . . . teacher-researchers . . . use action research to improve circumstances and understandings of personal, professional, and political dimensions. (pp. 10–11)

PITFALLS TO AVOID

Action research is demanding, time-consuming, and challenging. Perhaps the biggest difference between scientific research and action research is the role of the researcher. In scientific research, the researcher conducts the research and reports the findings. In action research, the researcher conducts the research and then is responsible for enacting the change. This dual role intensifies the full implementation of action research.

Start Small and Stay Focused

To recognize this dual undertaking, modest beginnings are preferable to more ambitious undertakings. Those who are new to action research or teaching are encouraged to start small and with a focused area. The time needed to conduct a study, and then to implement an action plan, are commonly misjudged by inexperienced teachers.

Caitlin was interested in involving her students with discussion strategies that would enhance class discussions in reading. She recognized that her students seemed bored with her typical approach to discussion—e.g., read the text and respond to teacher-generated questions in a whole class format.

In researching the topic, Caitlin found Brookfield and Preskill's (2005) research-based discussion strategies and decided to introduce five different strategies in a two-week period. She determined to take one day to teach a strategy, and the next day to let students use the strategy in the class discussion. At the end of the two-week period, she surveyed students on their preferred discussion strategy. Once she reviewed the surveys and found that there were multiple preferred strategies, she could not determine what to do next.

Caitlin's situation describes what happens when the researcher tries to do too much all at once. Several issues caused Caitlin to experience a roadblock in her action research.

Caitlin was more focused on students picking a favorite strategy than on the actual problem of those students who were not actively engaged in class discussions. She also tried to teach students five discussion strategies in a very short period of time. Students had one experience with each of the five new discussion strategies—provided they were present for class each day during the two-week period to learn the strategy and then to practice it. The student survey could have resulted in a popularity contest more than an academic approach to deciding on effectiveness of discussion strategies.

If Caitlin had perhaps focused on two strategies over a longer period of time, she may have had better results. Devising a research question, as she examined the problem with students' limited or bored participation, would help her focus the study.

Questions that are too broad—such as, what are students' favorite discussion strategies—often fail to help the researcher address the situation. While wanting to give students autonomy in a class discussion is a noble goal, she found that focusing research to address the problem will merit greater results. A revised question moved Caitlin closer to addressing her original problem: Which discussion strategy—snowballing or hatful of quotes—would be most appropriate for discussing this text?

Controlling for Variables

Another pitfall teachers experience when undertaking action research is including too many variables. This was an issue that Maita experienced (chapter 10) in working with students in the after-school math club.

Not only did Maita try to introduce the KWSL strategy to students in solving the homework problems, but she also was contending with (1) other tutors who were unfamiliar with the strategy, (2) students who did not have regular attendance, and (3) multiple math topics during the time period of her study. To determine the effectiveness of her KWSL strategy, these other variables had to be controlled. Using her strategy in the after-school club was a good idea for helping these students, but she needed a more regular group of students with whom she worked for a longer period of time to more effectively determine if the KWSL strategy worked.

Data Collection without Analysis

The purpose of collecting data in a study is to interpret and transform the data into credible evidence to support or give insight into the planned intervention. A simple question that can help in this process is, what does this information tell one about the intervention? Is there a difference because of the intervention, and how big a difference or change is there?

Dealing with data is a challenge in the regular classroom setting. Keeping up with entering student grades in a required grade-book program may be difficult for new teachers. Data need to be regarded as helpful information in all its aspects.

Teachers can be tempted to dump the data and draw general conclusions about the study. The data in action research—for new teachers without statistical backgrounds—should be kept simple and should definitely be used and reviewed. Simple data collections—that include such information as homework quality and test results—need to be understood by all teachers.

Too often those new to research miss an opportunity to organize data in a meaningful way. Using a spreadsheet can be especially helpful for "looking" at data. Elizabeth was using sprint activity sheets with her students to increase their math fluency. Students participated in the sprint exercise two days a week over the course of a semester. Using her spreadsheet with coded IDs for her students, she recorded the student scores on the two exercises for each day (table 12.1). Within two and a half weeks with consistent data entry, Elizabeth started noting some patterns in her students' scores.

Looking at the initial score (A) in the exercise and comparing it with the second round (B) for each day, Elizabeth noticed that almost every student had a higher second score than the first, which showed positive improved achievement. She also noted that the next day of the exercise, most students scored higher than they did on the initial sprint the day before.

With the maximum score at 40 in the sprint exercise, Elizabeth also found that students four, ten, and eleven were starting to hit that mark. If

Table 12.1. Student Sprint Scores

	Day 1		Day 2		Day 3		Day 4		Day 5	
	A	B	A	B	A	B	A	B	A	B
1	2	5	4	9	11	15	16	16	19	28
2	6	8	9	16	14	21	18	23	22	25
3	16	29	18	22	19	22	23	28	22	28
*4	13	14	20	21	22	36	33	39	35	40
5	14	14	16	25	17	23	23	29	23	28
6	11	20	9	16	4	14	15	20	—	—
7	9	5	11	13	—	—	12	19	22	24
8	5	17	14	19	14	25	21	26	20	28
9	7	17	9	17	10	22	15	25	19	28
*10	8	26	15	22	20	34	30	37	34	40
*11	14	19	13	19	19	33	28	36	40	40

this exercise was to be continued for the next seven weeks of the semester, she would need to decide if these students should continue the exercise, be challenged with the next level, or had reached the intended goal.

Elizabeth's daily recording of data allowed her to note what the data were telling her as she moved through her action research. If she had waited to record and analyze the data at the end of the semester, she would have missed opportunities to adjust her plan as the study progressed.

By the end of the semester, Elizabeth had enough data to answer questions and to interpret and analyze the data for meaning. She probably had enough data to gather other information on these students, but for the sake of the study, she reviewed the data only in light of student growth through these exercises.

Keeping Findings a Secret

One aspect of action research that is sometimes ignored is the sharing of results. Teacher researchers can generally be so happy when they have finished their research that they make changes to their own practice but dismiss its importance to other teachers. Or, as is the case with most assigned research at the graduate and undergraduate levels, the research is relegated to a spot on the shelf and never considered again.

Sharing action research findings holds an important place in the professional life of teachers. Findings from a study can contribute to dialogue and collaboration among educators within the school and beyond. The research contributes to the profession. The research improves student learning, which is the ultimate goal of all action research, and revises practices based on new findings.

Sharing the findings gives the teacher a voice that can be heard in schoolwide planning, in developing policies, and in bringing new insights to the teaching and learning process. Results found but never used beyond one setting remain buried treasures. "The researcher makes research public and shares findings in order to reflect upon new theory and emerging practice, process activities, and communicate development both on paper and via conversations, presentations, and reports completed as part of the professional role" (Ryan, 2013, p. 2).

Stick to Learning Matters

One final note of caution for the new researcher: avoid studies on matters one cannot change. We cannot change marital status and family structures of students' lives; we cannot change their socioeconomic status either. Don't try—and do not use these issues as the basis for action research.

Studies on these issues are relegated to another level—perhaps in graduate research courses or in doctoral studies. These societal issues may (and most likely do) have an impact on students' experiences. And while the information on participants in the study may include these issues, action research is not the way to study these issues.

The purpose of action research in education is to improve the lives of children and to learn about the craft of teaching. Action research examines classroom teaching principles and the effect of teachers' action on the children entrusted to their care (Mills, 2014). The focus is on improving learning and teaching. With that focus in mind, any action research study that is undertaken needs to remain focused on the teaching and learning process and those who are directly involved in the process. For those in beginning stages of action research, stick to matters that will make a difference in the classroom and in student learning.

BEGIN WITH THE END IN MIND

Habit 2 in Stephen Covey's *The 7 Habits of Highly Effective People* (1989) states "Begin with the end in mind." Covey talks about the vision each person creates:

> Habit 2 is based on imagination—the ability to envision in your mind what you cannot at present see with your eyes. It is based on the principle that all things are created twice. There is a mental (first) creation, and a physical (second) creation. The physical creation follows the mental, just as a building follows a blueprint. If you don't make a conscious effort to visualize who you

are and what you want in life, then you empower other people and circumstances to shape you and your life by default. (p. 147)

The same can be said of teachers who use action research to study their own practice and to improve student learning. Teachers imagine what can be (the first creation) and then take steps in action research to make it happen (the second creation). To teach is to learn. Learning is ongoing. Just as Covey suggests that Habit 2 is based on imagination, so are teaching and learning. The imagination is boundless, inexhaustible, and immeasurable.

Action research is invaluable in using the imagination for what is possible for making a difference in the lives of students and teachers. This book is just a beginning for what lies ahead in the imagination of every teacher who recognizes that what I know today is only a small part of what can be tomorrow.

Action research has the potential to transform teachers into effective practitioners. It is the step along the pathway to self-reflective inquiry and the development of highly qualified and competent teachers.

L.E.A.D.E.R. can be used in every area of the educational process—by students, parents, administrators—and very appropriately by teachers. Using *L.E.A.D.E.R.* as the steps to action research creates possibilities beyond the imagination.

As our action research journey begins and continues, teachers make the difference in the lives—the hearts and minds—of children, and it is the teacher who will transform learning. Take the steps, move forward, and let classrooms become those beyond-imagination places of unfathomable learning.

REFERENCES

Brookfield, S. D., & Preskill, S. (2005). *Discussion as a way of teaching: Tools and techniques for a democratic classroom.* (2nd ed.) San Francisco, CA: Jossey-Bass.

Brydon-Miller, M., Greenwood, D., & Maguire, P. (2003). Why action research? *Action Research, 1*(1), 9–28.

Carnegie Unit (2013, August 29). In S. Abbott (Ed.), *The glossary of education reform.* Retrieved from http://edglossary.org/carnegie-unit/.

Casey, A. (2012). A self-study using action research: Changing site expectations and practice stereotypes. *Educational Action Research, 20*(2), 219–232. doi:10.108 0/09650792.2012.676287

Covey, S. R. (1989). *The 7 habits of highly effective people: Powerful lessons in personal change.* New York, NY: Simon & Schuster Adult Publishing Group.

Giguere, M. (2015). Dance education action research: A twin study. *Research in Dance Education, 16*(1), 16–32.

Hagevik, R., Aydeniz, M., & Rowell, G. C. (2012). Using action research in middle level teacher education to evaluate and deepen reflective practice. *Teaching and Teacher Education: An International Journal of Research and Studies, 28*(5), 675–684.

Jordan, J., Perry, E., & Bevins, S. (2011). Is anyone listening? Action research and science teacher voice. *Education in Science, 242,* 12–13.

Kemmis, S. (2010). Research for praxis: Knowing doing. *Pedagogy, Culture & Society, 18*(1), 9–27.

Kemmis, S. (2011). Researching educational praxis: Spectator and participant perspectives. *British Educational Research Journal, 38*(6), 885–905.

Kemmis, S., & Grootenboer, P. (2008). Situating praxis in practice: Practice architectures and the cultural, social and material conditions for practice. In *Enabling praxis: Challenges for education,* ed. S. Kemmis and T. J. Smith, 37–62. Rotterdam: Sense.

Lattimer, H. (2012). Action research in pre-service teacher education: Is there value added? *i.e.: Inquiry in Education, 3*(1), 1–25.

Mills, G. E. (2014). *Action Research: A guide for the teacher researcher* (5th ed.). New York: Pearson.

Pine, G. J. (2009). *Teacher action research: Building knowledge democracies.* Thousand Oaks, CA: Sage. doi: http://dx.doi.org/10.4135/9781452275079

Ryan, T. G. (2013). The scholarship of teaching and learning within action research: Promise and possibilities. *i.e.: inquiry in education, 4*(2), 1–17. Retrieved from http://digitalcommons.nl.edu/ie/vol4/iss2/3.

Sagor, R. (2005). *The action research guidebook: A four=step process for educators and school teams.* Thousand Oaks, CA: Corwin Press.

Scientific Method. (n.d.), *American Heritage Dictionary of the English Language* (5th ed.). (2011). Retrieved July 11, 2015, from http://www.thefreedictionary.com/scientific+method.

Shute, J., & Cooper, B. S. (2014). *Fixing truancy now: Inviting students back to class.* Lanham, MD: Rowman & Littlefield.

Zambo, D. (2014). Theory in the service of practice: Theories in action research dissertations written by students in education doctorate programs. *Educational Action Research, 22*(4), 505–517.

Index

ABA. *See* American Bar Association

abstract, 89, 90–91, 92–93, 94

academic success, principals' vision of, 34–35

accountability, 27

achievement gap, 52

action research, 11–13, 157–68, *166*; definition, 41; dissemination, 106, 129–38, *132, 135–36,* 166–67; examples, 141–55, *147, 148, 149, 150, 151, 152, 155*; as focused, 163–64; insights, 155; knowledge acquired through, 85–94, *89, 93*; new teachers, 40–42; overview, 1, 94; pitfalls, 163–67, *166*; principals using, 40–42; principles, 27, *28*; research incorporated into, 94; samples, 141–55, *147, 148, 149, 150, 151, 152, 155*; as small, 163–64. *See also* cyclical action research

Action Research International, 133

Action Research: Teachers as Researchers in the Classroom (Mertler), 123

adding up, 42

administrators, 31–33, 35–38, 102–3, 129–30. *See also* principals

affective tone, 82

African American students, 49

after-school study program, 146–55, *147, 148, 149, 150, 151, 152, 155*

AMA. *See* American Medical Association

American Bar Association (ABA), 17

American Medical Association (AMA), 17

analysis, data collection without, 165–66, *166*

Anderson, S. E., 36–37

anticipated results, 106

applied research, teaching profession, 19–21, *20*

area of focus, 68, 145–46

argument, 88, *89,* 89–91

arrangement, 78

ASCD. *See* Association for Supervision and Curriculum Development

assessment, 151–52, *152,* 153–54

assignments, 81–82, 117

Association for Supervision and Curriculum Development (ASCD), 32–33

Association of American Colleges and Universities, 49

Atkeson, S., 96

attendance, 81, 117, 150, *151*
audience awareness, 129–30
Aydeniz, M., 161–62

Bacharach, Samuel, 19
background, 105
background sources, 87
background sources, exhibits,
    argument, methods (BEAM), 86–88
Behavior Event Interview (BEI), 75
behaviors, 78–79, *82*, 82–83
BEI. *See* Behavior Event Interview
Benigni, Mark D., 96
Berger, Ron, 80
best practices, 114
Bevins, S., 162
bilingual teachers, 91–94, *93*
Bill and Melinda Gates Foundation, 23
biology, 86–94, *89*, *93*, 141–55, *147*, *148*,
    149, *150*, *151*, *152*, *155*
Bizup, Joseph, 86–88
Blair, Leslie Asher, 103
Bondy, E., 76
Bozeman, L., 22
Brazil, 143–44
Brookfield, S. D., 164
Brown, J., 102
Brown, Jerry, 101
Brown, Richie, 18
Bruewer, A., 133
Buckingham, B. R., 15
"Building Better Teachers" (Green and
    Brown, J.), 102

Cain Project in Engineering and
    Professional Communication, 134
California, 101
Canada, 144–45
Carnegie Foundation for the
    Advancement of Teaching, 50
Carnegie Unit, 160–61
Carrejo, D. J., 91–94, *93*
Carver, C. L., 33
Center for Collaborative Action
    Research, 133
Charter Facilities Matching Grant
    Program, 40

chemistry, 117
class, 81–82
class climate, 35–36, 62–66, *65*, *67*,
    76–77, *77*
Classroom Climate Inventory, 77
classroom management. *See*
    management
classroom performance, systems
    model, 62–63, *63*
classroom rules. *See* rules
classrooms, 12–13; environment,
    26–27; happenings, 159–61;
    improving, 17–28, *20*, *28*; leaders,
    36; life, 17–28, *20*, *28*; physical
    arrangement, 78; procedures,
    79; records, 81; teachers paying
    attention to, 159–61
Clayton, J. K., 56
climate. *See* class climate
clinical experiences, 50
clinical work, 49–50
Code of Federal Regulations for the
    Protection of Human Subjects (45
    CFR 46), 119
codes of conduct, 119
Collaborative Action Research
    Network, 133
College Board, 24
colleges, 49
collegial interactions, 18
Collins, Jim, 34, 36
Columbia University, 103
Common Core State Standards, 113
community, classrooms, curriculum
    (3Cs), 100–101
community colleges, 49
competencies, 74–75
comprehensive assessment system, 120
concept mapping, 144–45
Connecticut, 96
control groups, 117
Cooper, B. S., 160
Cornell notes, 7, *8*
Cornell University, 40
Covey, Stephen, 167–68
Crawford, V., 22
Creswell, J. W., 86, *89*, 127–28

critical mass, 23
cyclical action research: dissemination, 129–38, *132*, *135–36*; findings, 129–38, *132*, *135–36*; learning, 123–24; poster, 133–38, *135–36*; presentation, 137–38; questions, 124–26, *126*; repeating, 138

Danielson, C., 14, 26, 74
data: analyzing, 99, 152–53; collection, 146–49, *147*, *148*, *149*, *150*, 165–66, *166*; from control groups, 117; effectiveness, 152–53; from experimental groups, 117; plan evaluated with, 117–19; principals managing, 38–39; strategies, 152–53
decision making, 38, 39
Dekas, K. H., 80
department chairs, 36
Department of Labor, U.S., 51–52
Design Professionalism (Rutledge), 19
direct characterization, 83
disengaged workers, 80
dissemination, 106, 129–38, *132*, *135–36*, 166–67
district leaders, 37
Dixon, A. J., 57
Dodson, Fitzhugh, 100
Duncan, Arne, 96
Dunning, David, 40
Dunning-Kruger effect, 40

Ed in the Apple, 40
EdSource, 101
"*EdSource*—Highlighting Strategies for Student Success" (EdSource), 101
education: climate, 35–36; development, 21; principals, 35–36; professionalism in, 18; schools, 103
Educational Action Research, 133
educational research. *See* research
Education Resource Information Center (ERIC), 32–33
elementary teachers, 73
ELLs. *See* English language learners
emotional setting, 79
England, 21–22

English class, 61–62
English language learners (ELLs), 91–94, *93*
environment, 26–27
ERIC. *See* Education Resource Information Center
ethical codes of conduct, 119
Etzioni, Amitai, 18, 19
European Education Research Association, 100–101
evaluation, 32, 111–20, *116*, 119–20
evidence information, 87–88
examining: behavior, 78–79; class climate, 76–77, *77*; expectations, 81–83, *82*; known, 73–83, *77*, *82*; management, 78–79; research, 85–94, *89*, *93*; students, 75–76, 83; teacher competence, 74–75; teacher practice, 73–74; work, 79–81
excellence gap, 52
execution, 111–20, *116*
exhibit information, 87–88
expectations, 66–68, *67*, 81–83, *82*
Expeditionary Learning Schools, 80
experience, 50, 73, 74
experimental design, 106
experimental groups, 117

faculty. *See Looking at problem, examining known, acquiring new knowledge and methods for handling problems, devising plan, executing and evaluating plan, repeating steps as needed*
faculty meetings, 35, 37
Feiman-Nemser, S., 22
female jobs, 18
Ferrance, Eileen, 3
field notes, 118
final products, 106
findings, 129–38, *132*, *135–36*
first-year teachers, 85
fixing up, 43
flying up, 43
focus, 68, 163–64
Fordham University, 24–25
formal organization, in systems model, 62, 64–66, *65*, *67*

Forsyth, P., 62
45 CFR 46. *See* Code of Federal
    Regulations for the Protection of
    Human Subjects
fourth-graders, 25, 160
Framework for Teaching, 14
Fraser, B. J., 76–77
Fusco, J., 22

Gallup Inc., 80
garbage, 53–54
gender, 18
geometry, 106–9
Germany, 114
Giguere, Miriam, 158
Ginnot, Haim, 26
goals, 100, 103, 105, 115–16, *116*
Goldman Sachs, 40
Goldman Sachs Gives, 40
Goldys, Pat, 42
Goodnough, K., 111
Good to Great (Collins), 34
grades, 81
graduates, 103
graduate students, 24–25
graduation, student, 49
graphic notes, 7–8
Green, Elizabeth, 102, 103, 104
Grootenboer, P., 161
Grossen, Bonnie, 32
guardians, 54, 130
guide questions, 91–92, 94

Hagevik, R., 161–62
Harlem Children's Zone (HCZ), 40
Harvard University, 75
Haycock, Katie, 55–56
HCZ. *See* Harlem Children's Zone
Heath, Chip, 114
Heath, Dan, 114
hedgehog model, 36
Hiebert, James, 114
high-expectancy students, *82*, 82–83
high-income households, 23
high school students: biology, 86–94,
    89, *93*, 141–55, *147*, *148*, *149*, *150*,

151, *152*, *155*; English class, 61–62;
    geometry, 106–9; learning, 11–12;
    math lab, 125–28, *126*; notes, 4–12,
    6, *8*, *9*, *10*; reading, 3–4, 5, 7, *8*, 8–10,
    9, 11–12, 83; science, 115–16, *116*,
    118–19; U.S. history class, 4–7, *6*, 8,
    9, 10, *10*, 12, 83; writing, 3–4, 5, 7, *8*,
    8–10, *9*, 11–12, 83
high school teachers, 73
Hill, L. H., 75
history class, 4–7, *6*, 8, 9, 10, *10*, 12
Hord, Shirley, 103
Hosseini, Khaled, 3–4, *8*, 8–10, *9*
Hoy, W. K., 62
humanities, 11–12, 13
Hyland, T., 76

imagination, 167–68
Indiana Historical Society, *6*
indirect characterization, 83
induction program, 22–23, 33
inscriptions, 143–44
instruction, principals, 37–38
Instructional Assessment Resources,
    97
interactions with students, 82–83

Jamison, S., 155
Japan, 102, 114
Jordan, J., 162

Keen, S., 129
Kemmis, S., 58–59, 161
The Kite Runner (Hosseini), 3–4, *8*,
    8–10, *9*
knowledge, 7–8, 73–83, *77*, *82*, 85–94,
    89, *93*
Koch, M., 22
Kruger, Justin, 40
Kuh, G. D., 14, 50
KWSL chart. *See* what I Know, what I
    Want to know, possible Source of
    information, what I Learned chart

language, 55, 91–94, *93*
Latino students, 49

Lattimer, H., 158
LCFF. *See* Local Control Funding
  Formula
*L.E.A.D.E.R. See Looking at problem,
  examining known, acquiring new
  knowledge and methods for handling
  problems, devising plan, executing
  and evaluating plan, repeating steps as
  needed*
leaders, 36, 37, 56–58, 63
leadership, 32–33, 34, 35, 36–37, 39–41
Leadership Academy, 40
learning: action research, 123–24;
  administrators, 35–36; high school
  students, 11–12; levels of, 123;
  matters, 167; principals, 35–36; from
  research problem, 124; student
  process, 76; teachers influencing,
  26–27
Lee, Harper, 66–70, *67*
legal codes of conduct, 119
Lehman, P., 22
Leithwood, K., 36–37
lesson plans, 118
Levine, Arthur, 103
life outcomes, 26–27
life skills, 38
limitations, 127
linear notes, 7–8
Lipsky, 100–101
Local Control Funding Formula
  (LCFF), 101
long division, 25
*Looking at problem, examining known,
  acquiring new knowledge and methods
  for handling problems, devising
  plan, executing and evaluating
  plan, repeating steps as needed
  (L.E.A.D.E.R.),* 124, 137–38, 155,
  168; on daily basis, 54–55; example,
  53–54, 141–55, *147, 148, 149, 150,
  151, 152, 155*; following, 58–59;
  implementing, 54; introducing,
  53; overview, 47, 49–59; steps, 52,
  58–59; teachers as, 55–56
Lortie, Daniel C., 18

Louis, K. S., 36–37
low-expectancy students, *82*, 82–83
low-income households, 23

"Making Policy in the Classroom"
  (European Education Research
  Association), 100–101
management, 78–79
Marzano, R. J., 32–33, 82
master teachers, 75
matching up, 42
math, 23, 125–28, *126*, 164–66, *166*
McClelland, David, 75
McEwan, Elaine, 56
McLaughlin, M., 108
McLaughlin, M. W., 18
McNulty, B. A., 32–33
medium, 130–33, *132*
men, 18
mentoring, 22–23, 33
Meriden, Connecticut, 96
Merriam-Webster, Inc., 18–19
Merriam-Webster's Dictionary
  (Merriam-Webster, Inc.), 18–19
Mertler, C. A., 123
methods, 88
Microsoft, 134
middle school teachers, 73
Mills, G. E., 41, 68, 118, 133
Ministry of Education (MOE), 75
mismatch, 66–68, *67*
MOE. *See* Ministry of Education
Montreal High School, 144–45
Mosle, S., 104

NAEP. *See* National Assessment of
  Education Progress
narrative response, 69
National Assessment of Education
  Progress (NAEP), 52
National Association of Elementary
  School Principals, 39
needs, 100–101
Nellie Mae Education Foundation, 96
Networks, 133
New Jersey, 51, 96

new teachers: action research, 40–42; behavior, 78–79; first-year, 85; management, 78–79; need for, 103; principals influencing, 31–43; problems, 33, 40; profession left by, 33; research, 85–86; students learned about by, 74, 75–76. *See also* teacher candidates

New York, 96, 112–13

New York City, 102, 113

New York City Department of Education, 40

nonlinear notes, 8

North Carolina, 18

notes, 83; abstract, 90–91; field, 118; high school students, 4–12, *6, 8, 9, 10*

Obama, Barack, 40, 96

objectives, 105

OECD. *See* Organisation for Economic Co-operation and Development

Olshavsky, J. E., 143

online surveys, 59

Organisation for Economic Co-operation and Development (OECD), 21

The Organization Man (Whyte), 34

paired questioning strategy, 148–49, *149, 150*

parents, 54, 130

participants, 92, 145, 158–59

PBS NewsHour, 102–3

peer review, 70–71

people, 38–39

Perry, E., 162

Phillips, M., 22

Phillips, V., 23

photographs, 143–44

physical arrangement, 78

physical setting, 79

PIE. *See Planning, Implementing, Evaluating*

Pine, G. J., 163

planning, 95–96, 96–104, *97, 98–99*, 100, 103

Planning, Implementing, Evaluating (PIE), 97–99, *98–99*

plans: data, 117–19; devising, 95–109, *97, 98–99*; evaluating, 111–20, *116*; executing, 111–20, *116*; finalizing, 103; goals, 103; improvement, 114; issues, 119–20; plans compared with, 104; proposal, 104–9; resources, 103. *See also* specific, measurable, attainable, realistic, time driven goals

Policy Link, 40

Polush, E., 133

poster, 133–38, *135–36*

PowerPoint, 134

Pozzer, L., 143–44

practices, 5, 7–8, 31–43, 161–62. *See also* teacher practices

presentation, 137–38

Preskill, S., 164

primary source analysis worksheet, *6, 9, 10, 10*

principals, 103; academic success vision, 34–35; action research used by, 40–42; climate, 35–36; data managed by, 38–39; decision making, 38; education, 35–36; instruction, 37–38; leadership, 32–33, 34, 36–37; learning, 35–36; new teachers influenced by, 31–43; people managed by, 38–39; practices improved by, 31–43; processes managed by, 38–39; role, 31–43; school improvement, 37–38; trust, 36

problems: checking, 70–71; focusing on, 63–64; getting to, 67–68; guide question, 91–92; learning from, 124; looking at, 61–71, *63, 65, 67*; narrative response, 69; new teachers, 33, 40; overview, 61–71, *63, 65, 67*; peer review, 70–71; research questions, 68–70; sample, 61–71, *63, 65, 67*; as solved, 124; statement of, 105; teachers, 5, 7, 23–24, 27, *28* problem solvers, 51–52. *See also Looking at problem, examining known, acquiring new knowledge and methods for handling problems, devising plan, executing and evaluating plan, repeating steps as needed*

problem solving, 51, 52, 55, 59. *See also Looking at problem, examining known, acquiring new knowledge and methods for handling problems, devising plan, executing and evaluating plan, repeating steps as needed*

procedures, 79, 92, 146

profession, 18–19

professional development, 23, 35

professionalism, 18, 19, 27

professional learning communities, 131

Professional Responsibilities, 14

project, 105, 106, 108

Promise Neighborhood Institute, 40

Promise Neighborhoods initiative, 40

proposal, 104–9

purpose, 68, 145

Quebec, Canada, 144–45

Race to the Top, 96

Rand Corporation, 27, *28*

reading: fluency, 117; high school students, 3–4, 5, 7, *8*, 8–10, *9*, 11–12, 83; strategies, 141–55, *147*, *148*, *149*, *150*, *151*, *152*, *155*

reality, 66–68, *67*

records, 81

Reflecting on Teaching, 14

reflective analysis, 50

reflective piece, 61–62

reflective practice, 161–62

Reflective Practice, 133

reflective thinking, 14–15, 119

reform, 101, 103

Reinhartz, J., 91–94, *93*

repeating, 123–38, *126*, *132*, *135–36*

research, 13; action research incorporated into, 94; articles, 35;

examining, 85–94, *89*, *93*; example, 86–94, *89*, *93*; finding, 85–86; knowledge, 7–8; new teacher, 85–86; overview, 94; practices, 7–8; preparation, 7–8; on research, 157–68, *166*

research problem. *See* problems

research questions, 68–70, 91–92, 105

resources, 101, 103

responsibility, 27

retirement, 24–25

Rhode Island Department of Education, 120

Riel, M., 133

Ross, D. D., 76

Rosso, B. D., 80

Roth, W. M., 143–44

Rowell, G. C., 133, 161–62

rules, 78

Rutledge, Andy, 19, *20*, 27

Ryan, T. G., 163

safety, 78

Sagor, R., 25

salaries, 18, 25

sample problem, 61–71, *63*, *65*, *67*

sample proposal, 106–9

Sanders, William, 23

Sawchuk, Stephen, 112

Schlager, M., 22

Schmid, R. F., 144–45

school districts, administrators influencing, 37–38

school improvement, 37–38, 95–109, *97*, *98–99*

"School Leadership That Works, from Research to Results" (Marzano, Waters, and McNulty), 32–33

schools, 26–27, 35, 103

Schoolteacher: A Sociological Inquiry (Lortie), 18

science high school, 115–16, *116*, 118–19

science teachers, 113–14

science tests, 117

scientific method, 158–59

searches, 88
self-reflection, 119
semiprofession, 17–18
semiprofessionals, 17–18, 19
*The Semi-Professions and Their
    Organization* (Etzioni and Lortie), 18
Serpell, Z., 22
Seven Habits of Highly Effective People
    (Covey), 167–68
Shedd, Joseph, 19
Shulman, Lee, 50
Shute, J., 160
silent curriculum, 27
Singapore model, 75
Siudock, Joseph, 102–3
SMART goals. *See* specific,
    measurable, attainable, realistic,
    time driven goals
Socratic seminar, 62–70, *63*, *65*, *67*
Soprano, K., 113–14
Spanish, 115–16, *116*, 118–19
specific, measurable, attainable,
    realistic, time driven (SMART)
    goals, 114, 115–16, *116*
staff, 102–3. *See also Looking at problem,
    examining known, acquiring new
    knowledge and methods for handling
    problems, devising plan, executing
    and evaluating plan, repeating steps
    as needed*
Stanford Diagnostic Reading Test,
    144–45
State Education Law 3012c, 113
statement, 105
Stigler, James, 114
*Strategies for Success: Implementing a
    Successful School Reform Program*
    (Blair), 103
student achievement, leadership
    influencing, 35. *See also* academic
    success
student learning. *See* learning
student performance, leadership
    improving, 39–41. *See also* student
    achievement
students, 12–13; college, 49;
    decision making influenced by,
    39; developing, 76; examining,
    75–76, 83; graduation, 49; high-
    expectancy, *82*, 82–83; interactions
    with, 82–83; knowledge, 75–76, 83;
    leaders, 63; learning process, 76;
    low-expectancy, *82*, 82–83; new
    teachers learning about, 74, 75–76;
    outcome quality, 26–27; relevance,
    79–81; responses, 151; safety
    influencing, 78; in systems model,
    62; teachers learning about, 83;
    value, 79–81; work, 79–81, 146–49,
    147, *148*, *149*, *150*. *See also* academic
    success; African American
    students; high school students;
    Latino students; *Looking at problem,
    examining known, acquiring new
    knowledge and methods for handling
    problems, devising plan, executing
    and evaluating plan, repeating steps
    as needed*; problem solving
student teaching, 112
study, 89–90, 125–28, *126*, 141–55, *147*,
    148, *149*, *150*, *151*, *152*, *155*
study group, 102
studying, 13, 73–74
subjects, 92
superintendent, 103
supervisor, 129
surveys, 59
Swanson, Beverly, 100
*Switch: How to Change Things When
    Change Is Hard* (Heath and Heath),
    114
systems model, 62–70, *63*, *65*, *67*

Talbert, J. E., 18
Tangled Hierarchies (Shedd and
    Bacharach), 19
TARC model. *See* Teacher Action
    Research Cluster model
task, in systems model, 62, 64–66, *65*, *67*
Teacher Action Research Cluster
    (TARC) model, 163
teacher candidates, 49–50, 73–74
teacher practices, 13; examining,
    73–74; examples, 3–12, *6*, *8*, *9*, *10*;

improvement, 3–15, *6, 8, 9, 10;*
knowledge, 7–8, 73–74; overview,
3–15, *6, 8, 9, 10;* plan, *8,* 8–10, *9, 10;*
problem, 5, 7; research, 7–8; stories,
3–12, *6, 8, 9, 10*
teacher preparation: challenges,
5, 7; examples, 3–12, *6, 8, 9, 10;*
improvement, 3–15, *6, 8, 9, 10;*
knowledge, 7–8; overview, 3–15,
6, 8, 9, 10; plan, *8,* 8–10, *9, 10;*
problem, 5, 7; research, 7–8; science,
113–14; stories, 3–12, *6, 8, 9, 10*
teachers: as administrators, 102–3;
administrators' relationship with,
31–33; as artists, 25; behaviors,
82, 82–83; best practices for, 114;
bilingual, 91–94, *93;* classroom
attention of, 159–61; competence,
74–75; comprehensive assessment
system, 120; decision making, 38;
elementary, 73; emotional setting
examined by, 79; environment
influenced by, 26–27; expectations,
81–83, *82;* first-year, 85; graduates,
103; high school, 73; induction
program, 22–23, 33; leaders, 36,
56–58; as *L.E.A.D.E.R.S,* 55–56;
learning influenced by, 26–27;
lives, 17–28, *20, 28;* mentoring,
22–23; middle school, 73; mindset, 19; overview, 17–18; physical
setting examined by, 79; plateau,
112; problems, 5, 7, 23–24, 27,
28; professional development,
23, 35; quality, 112–13; reflective
thinking, 14–15; retirement, 24–25;
rules developed by, 78; safety
considered by, 78; salaries, 18, 25;
science, 113–14; as scientists, 25;
as semiprofessionals, 17–18, 19;
shortages, 21–22; students learned
about by, 83; study group, 102;
studying, 13; in systems model, 62;
teachers watched by, 102; teaching,
111–12; undergraduate research,
11–12, 14–15; understanding, 17–28,

20, 28; voice, 162–63; as warm
demanders, 76. *See also Looking at
problem, examining known, acquiring
new knowledge and methods for
handling problems, devising plan,
executing and evaluating plan,
repeating steps as needed;* master
teachers; new teachers; plans;
research; teacher candidates;
teacher practices; training
Teachers College, 103
teacher-training programs, 103
teaching, 12, 19–26, *20,* 33, 111–12
*The Teaching Gap: Best Ideas from the
World's Teachers for Improving
Education in the Classroom* (Stigler
and Hiebert), 114
teaching-learning processes, 39
Telaro, G., 144–45
10 Traits of Highly Effective Teachers
(McEwan), 56–57
test scores, 117
textbooks, 143–44
Themes in Education: Action Research
(Ferrance), 3
3Cs. *See* community, classrooms,
curriculum
three-column strategy, *9*
timeline, 106, 108
Todres, L., 129
To Kill a Mockingbird (Lee), 66–70, *67*
tools, 92
training, 1, 112
truancy, 160
trust, principals, 36
tutoring program, 146–55, *147, 148,
149, 150, 151, 152, 155*

undergraduate level, 50
undergraduate research, teachers,
11–12, 14–15
unengaged workers, 80
United States (U.S.), 102, 114; history
class, 4–7, *6, 8, 9, 10, 10,* 12, 83;
teacher graduates, 103; workforce,
80

University of Minnesota, 35
University of Oregon, 32
University of Texas, Austin, 97
University of Toronto, 35
up is up, 43
upward process, 42–43

Vanderbilt Assessment of Leadership
    in Education, 39–40
Vanderbilt University, 39–40
variables, 35, 127, 164–65
VCEE approach. *See* vocabulary
    preview, concept outline, example,
    evidence approach
vision, 34–35, 167–68
visual representation, 106–9
vocabulary instruction, 117
vocabulary preview, concept outline,
    example, evidence (VCEE)
    approach, 117
voice, 162–63

Wahlstrom, K. L., 36–37
Wallace Foundation, 32, 37–38, 55–56
Wallace Perspective, 34
warm demanders, 76
Waters, T., 32–33
wcpm. *See* words correct per minute

what I Know, what I Want to know,
    possible Source of information,
    what I Learned (KWSL) chart,
    125–28, *126*, 147, 152–53
whole child, 75
Whyte, William, 34
Wilmington, North Carolina, 18
women, 18
Wong, Harry K., 22, 78
Wong, Rosemary, 78
Wooden, John, 141, 155
words correct per minute (wcpm),
    117
work: clinical, 49–50; examining,
    79–81; knowledge, 79–81; student,
    79–81, 146–49, *147*, *148*, *149*, *150*;
    teaching profession, 22–24; value,
    80–81
workers, 80
workforce, 80
writing, 50; high school students, 3–4,
    5, 7, *8*, 8–10, *9*, 11–12, 83; proposal,
    104–9; strategies, 143
Wrzesniewski, A., 80

Yang, L., 113–14

Zambo, D., 158

About the Authors

Sr. Mary Ann Jacobs, Ed.D., is an assistant professor in the School of Education at Manhattan College in Riverdale, New York. She prepares education majors to become teachers for middle and high school students. Her research interests include STEM education, brain-compatible instruction, and effective middle schools. She is a contributing author in *Mentoring with Meaning*, edited by Carlos McCray and Bruce S. Cooper, and *Using Technology in 21st Century Schools*, edited by William Merriman and Augustine Nicoletti.

Bruce S. Cooper, Ph.D., is professor emeritus at Fordham University, Graduate School of Education, with a focus on research, including (1) politics and policy in education, with his books *Better Policies, Better Schools* and *Handbook of Education Politics and Policy*; (2) private school religious education, with his book *Blurring the Lines* and "Finding a Golden Mean in Education Policy: Centering Religious and Public Schools," in the *Peabody Journal of Education*; and (3) fixing school problems, with his books *Fixing Truancy Now* with Jon Shute; *Truancy Revised* with Rita Guare; and *Mentoring with Meaning* with Carlos McCray.